Audio Access Included

VIOLIN AEROBICS

MW00830290

Contents

Introduction 2

Using This Book 2

About the Online Audio 3

Weeks 1–52: Exercises 1–365 4–108

Acknowledgments 109

About the Author... 109

To access audio visit:
www.halleonard.com/mylibrary
Enter Code
8353-3046-1603-3128

Cover Illustration by Birck Cox

ISBN 978-1-4803-7135-4

HAL•LEONARD®
CORPORATION

7777 W. BLUEMOUND RD. P.O. BOX 13819 MILWAUKEE, WI 53213

In Australia Contact:
Hal Leonard Australia Pty. Ltd.
4 Lentara Court
Cheltenham, Victoria, 3192 Australia
Email: ausadmin@halleonard.com.au

Visit Hal Leonard Online at
www.halleonard.com

INTRODUCTION

This book is written as a series of studies for the violinist or fiddler who's interested in popular music. Many of the exercises are useful for any violinist, but the book has been written with popular music as its focus. You'll be introduced to the bends and slides of the blues vocabulary. There are exercises that focus on getting a good rhythmic feel on fiddle tunes. There is a progression of exercises to teach you to swing. There are lots of funk lines, rock licks, some Latin figures, and so on.

The canon of studies and etudes for the violin is massive. There's nothing I could write that could improve on what's taught in books by Kreutzer, Flesch, Paganini, et al. But there is not much out there for the player who's interested in playing non-classical styles. Often, when classical violinists approach popular music, they sound unconvincing. Fiddlers trying to play jazz or jazz players trying to play rock can have the same difficulties. I've tried to assemble a collection of short studies that will help you to sound "right" playing different styles of music.

This book could be useful to a player at almost any level of experience. If you're just starting to play and need guidance with how to hold the instrument and bow, where the pitches are, etc., you'll want to look for a different resource to get yourself going. If you've played in a school strings program for a couple years or can play some basic scales and simple songs, you'll be able to start using this book. A lot of the playing techniques will be useful to a motivated player with modest experience. The book progresses fairly rapidly, though. If you're a relatively new player you might need to set the book aside for a bit and come back to it as you become more advanced.

A seasoned player will be able to dive right in. Don't skip the early exercises, even if they appear simple. There are some basic concepts there that are the key to making your playing sound convincing.

You'll be able to keep coming back to these etudes even after working through the entire book. You'll find yourself doing more with the music each time you revisit it and there are some basic exercises here that you'll never really outgrow.

I sincerely hope you enjoy this book. I believe there's a lot here to help you. I've improved my own playing by working on these exercises. I hope you will, too!

Best wishes,
Jon Vriesacker

USING THIS BOOK

The goal of this book is to give you a collection of etudes that improve your technique while giving you a framework of skills that will help you sound convincing playing popular music on the violin. You will be introduced to the basic vocabulary of pop music and given lots of opportunities to develop your sound in different genres. Use this book alongside traditional violin studies to expand your abilities into modern popular music.

There are several ways to approach these exercises. The template for this book is a lick-a-day resource for a year. You can begin on a Monday and work your way through the material, tackling a new problem every day. At the end of the year you will have conquered a huge number of licks and techniques. Or, if you have a particular interest that you'd like to explore, learning about chords for example, you could work your way through all the Thursday exercises first. Or you might enjoy just browsing through the book, working on whatever catches your fancy. Any of these approaches is fine. Work in whatever way keeps you excited about playing!

The most important thing you can do with this book is to focus on the recordings of the exercises. I've tried to be meticulous with the notation and thorough in the accompanying text, but listening attentively to the recordings and trying to copy the sounds you hear are the most significant steps you can take. There are elements of pop music that just aren't possible to convey in notation. Even if something seems self-explanatory, take a moment to listen to the example.

Many of the exercises lend themselves to being practiced as a repeating cycle. It can be hugely beneficial to put on a metronome or one of the included drum tracks and play an exercise as a repeating loop. (These drum tracks are divided into seven rhythm tracks, each one with a range of tempos. Each exercise lists which rhythm track to use.) You'll start hearing and improving parts of your playing that won't come to your attention if you play through the example only twice.

The exercises in this book are divided into seven categories, one for each day of the week. They begin with basic material and progress to some pretty flashy material by the end. Every player has different strengths and weaknesses. If you choose to work chronologically through the book, you may find yourself breezing through one category and struggling with another. There's no reason you have to wait to perfect an arpeggio before working on a blues example, for instance. Just put a check mark by the exercises you've done and take your time with the examples that really push you.

Monday's exercises focus on scales. We'll start with some basic material, but soon you will be conquering material that will challenge you technically while introducing you to some more sophisticated sounds. You'll learn what scales work with different chords, develop a foundation for improvising, and find what notes can add spice to otherwise bland melodies.

On **Tuesdays** we'll look at dozens of different techniques designed to announce that you're a legitimate player of pop music. You'll have a chance to study the inflections that can sound so effortless, but at first are difficult to mimic. We'll look at pitch bends, slides, ghost notes, and more.

Wednesdays are all about rhythm and the different feels of pop music. We'll work through the basics of learning to swing, giving a cool rhythmic lilt to fiddle tunes, articulating like a funk horn section, and so on.

On **Thursdays** you'll become facile with chords. We'll start with basic triads, explore seventh chords, and practice playing the chords you hear in jazz and other harmonically sophisticated styles.

Fridays provide a chance to develop licks and approaches that will help you to play with other people. You'll learn some examples of accompaniment figures and how to reinforce what other musicians are playing or singing.

Saturday's exercises focus on bowing techniques. You'll expand your repertoire of pop music articulations, push yourself with some advanced techniques, and learn about "chop" techniques that widen the boundaries of what the violin can do.

Sundays allow you to stretch out. Every week you'll have a chance to play an extended lick or a short tune that further develops the techniques you've practiced. These short pieces will give you an opportunity to put what you've learned into a musical context that will solidify your newfound skills.

Keep exploring with your ears and use this book to develop the skills to play the sounds that excite you!

ABOUT THE ONLINE AUDIO

On the title page of this book you will find a code that allows you to access the online rhythm tracks and demo tracks. You can listen to these online or download them.

There are seven rhythm tracks, each with a variety of practice tempos. At the top of each exercise, an appropriate rhythm track is noted; start slowly and increase the bpm (beats per minute) rate as you become more fluent with a given etude.

A demo track is available for each of the 365 exercises. These are named numerically, according to the workout number. For example, Wednesday of Week 3 is Workout #17.

MON

Workout #1   **Rhythm Track:** #2   **Technique:** Scales   **Genre:** Any

Description: Let's take a look at the major scale. This is probably familiar territory, but today as you play, pay attention to the distance (the interval) from each note to the next. The distance will be either a whole step (like from the first note to the second and the second note to third) or a half step (like from the third note to the fourth and the seventh note up to the root).

Tip: Now that you recognize the pattern used to construct a major scale, begin on other pitches. Some keys are more comfortable to play than others, but the pattern is always the same.

TUE

Workout #2   **Rhythm Track:** #2   **Technique:** Ornaments   **Genre:** Any pop style

Description: Today we'll play a slide between two pitches. We're sliding up to a neighboring note a half step higher.

Tip: First play the passage with the printed fingering, but without the slide. Once you're familiar with the notes, turn each pair of slurred notes into one smooth gesture. Be sure to listen to the recording.

WED

Workout #3   **Rhythm Track:** #4   **Technique:** Rhythm/Feel   **Genre:** Pop/Swing

Description: This is as simple-looking an exercise as one could want! The trick, though, is to make it feel good. Pay attention to your note lengths and accents, and compare them to the recording. Use a straight tone, one without vibrato.

Tip: Even with this one-pitch, quarter-note pattern, you want to communicate a swinging, danceable feel. Try playing both notated bowings. The top bowing is a basic swing bowing and starts up-bow to help bring out the accents on beats 2 and 4. More advanced players can practice the bottom bowing as well, with retakes between the notes.

Workout #4   **Rhythm Track:** #6   **Technique:** Arpeggios   **Genre:** Any

Description: A major chord is built by playing the first (root), third, and fifth notes of a major scale at the same time. An arpeggio is simply the notes of a chord played one at a time.

Tip: As you play this A major arpeggio, notice that you're playing the notes of Monday's A major scale, but leaving out some of the notes. Set your tuner to play a drone on A and concentrate on playing each note perfectly in tune.

Workout #5   **Rhythm Track:** #7   **Technique:** Playing with Others   **Genre:** Bluegrass

Description: A repeated rhythmic figure like this can really help to drive an ensemble. Sticking with one or two pitches helps you stay out of the way when the focus is on someone else.

Tip: Play the first bar until the accents are smooth and automatic. Think of the direction of the bow on the accented notes: down, down, up. In the second bar, play the accented notes by changing the angle of the bow only enough to add in the D string.

Workout #6   **Rhythm Track:** #5   **Technique:** Bowing   **Genre:** Any

Description: This exercise will help your string crossings to be clean and accurate. Be rhythmically precise as you play across the open strings.

Tip: If you're an advanced player, reverse the bowings (start up-bow). That will make the exercise more challenging.

Workout #7   **Rhythm Track:** #1   **Technique:** Stretching Out   **Genre:** Pop

About the Example: Listen to the recording to get a sense of how this example should sound. Pay attention to the note lengths and the minimal use of vibrato.

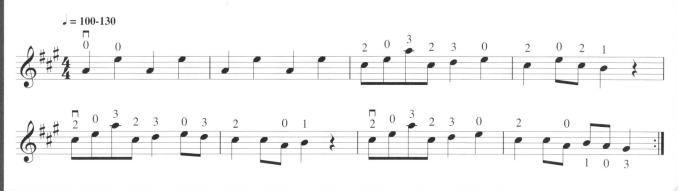

WEEK 2

MON

Workout #8   **Rhythm Track:** #2   **Technique:** Scales   **Genre:** Any

Description: A pentatonic scale is made of five notes. Major and minor pentatonic scales are very useful and are the foundation of tons of great popular music. Lots of popular melodies have been written using just these five notes. This is a G major pentatonic scale.

Tip: Try playing this scale in other keys. If you have trouble, play the major scale first, then leave out the fourth and seventh notes to form the pentatonic scale.

TUE

Workout #9   **Rhythm Track:** #2   **Technique:** Ornaments   **Genre:** Any pop style

Description: This excerpt highlights the tension between the ♭3 and ♮3 and the ♭5 and the ♮5 of the blues scale. It's also a good introduction to the bending of notes that is part of the blues style.

Tip: Begin by playing this with the written fingering, but without the slides. Then, on the slurred notes, slow the movement of your finger so that the sliding of each finger is audible. Finally, slide your finger so that each pair of notes is a single glissando. The recording will help you understand the gesture you're after.

WED

Workout #10   **Rhythm Track:** #4   **Technique:** Rhythm/Feel   **Genre:** Swing/Jazz

Description: This pattern of eighth notes will help you start to swing. On paper, swing eighth notes look identical to even eighth notes, but the word "swing" at the beginning of the exercise alerts the player that the rhythm isn't "straight." It's up to the player to interpret these swinging rhythms. Swung eighth notes are the basic rhythm of jazz and swing music.

Tip: There are lots of ways to swing. Instead of looking for a specific, precise rhythm, listen to how good jazz musicians play. Imitate them. You will immediately understand the basic idea by listening to the recording of this exercise. Then explore the music of lots of players and mimic the sounds that excite you.

THU

Workout #11   **Rhythm Track:** #6   **Technique:** Arpeggios   **Genre:** Any

Description: This C major arpeggio is played in first position, but with a twist. For the C on the E string, reach up with your pinkie beyond where you normally play.

Tip: When you reach up for that C, instead of shifting or sliding your hand up the neck, keep your second finger down and reach up with your third finger and pinkie. You'll be stretching just a tiny bit. There are lots of licks and passages that become much easier if you're comfortable with this small extension.

FRI

Workout #12   **Rhythm Track:** #2   **Technique:** Playing with Others   **Genre:** Funk/Pop

Description: When you're playing with other people, a simple, repetitive figure can keep things from sounding cluttered. As an accompanist, you want to leave plenty of room for other players to shine.

Tip: This simple figure is like a bass line. Play it rhythmically, without vibrato. It also works well played pizzicato. Find a friend to play along with you. Keep repeating this exercise as an accompaniment and let them improvise something. If there's a keyboard around, have them improvise some melodies by playing only the white keys.

SAT

Workout #13   **Rhythm Track:** #2   **Technique:** Bowing   **Genre:** Any pop style

Description: In pop music, notes are often held out and then ended abruptly. An organ does this articulation naturally. It's binary: the sound is on or off, like a switch. Funk horn sections clip the ends of notes like this all the time. As a string player, this gesture doesn't come naturally, but today we'll start to conquer it!

Tip: Begin each bow with a tiny accent and sustain it without dissipating the sound. No tapering, just on and then off, right on the next beat.

SUN

Workout #14   **Rhythm Track:** #1   **Technique:** Stretching Out   **Genre:** Pop

About the Example: If you're a classically trained player, it may be difficult at first to play without vibrato. A straight tone is the basic approach to most popular music, though, so start building this new habit as you practice today's exercise.

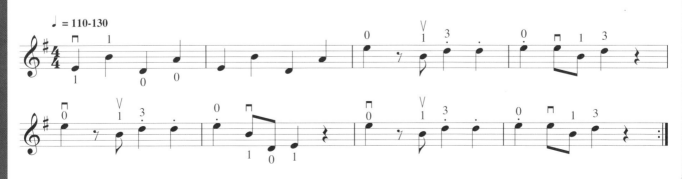

MON

Workout #15   **Rhythm Track:** #2   **Technique:** Scales   **Genre:** Any

Description: There are several kinds of minor scales. Today we'll play the natural minor. (Its pattern of whole and half steps is created by beginning on a major scale's sixth note.) This scale is commonly referred to as the relative minor of a major key or scale. The two keys share the same notes and key signature, but have a different sound because of which notes and chords are emphasized.

Tip: As you did with the major scale, pay attention to the pattern of whole steps and half steps. The pitches of the B natural minor scale are identical to those of the D major scale, but the sound is quite different.

TUE

Workout #16   **Rhythm Track:** #2   **Technique:** Ornaments   **Genre:** Any pop style

Description: Today we'll learn what's probably the most common ornament in pop music, a pitch bend. This short upward nudge of the pitch is something you'll use a lot.

Tip: This effect is powerful, but the distance that the pitch changes is small, about a quarter step. (In this example, that's only halfway to a D♯.) You may be tempted to move too far, so remember to keep the pitch change at a minimum.

WED

Workout #17   **Rhythm Track:** #4   **Technique:** Rhythm/Feel   **Genre:** Swing/Jazz

Description: Let's continue with our swing rhythms. Today we'll combine the eighth notes and quarter notes that we worked on in Weeks 1 and 2. As you repeat the exercise, the bowings will reverse.

Tip: Use a straight tone, without vibrato. You don't need to sustain the quarter notes for their full value. Listen to the online audio to get an idea of what you're going for. Even better, listen to the swinging-est violinist ever, Stuff Smith!

THU

Workout #18   **Rhythm Track:** #6   **Technique:** Arpeggios   **Genre:** Any

Description: The difference between a major arpeggio and a minor one is the second note. (Each note of an arpeggio is numbered according to where it falls in a scale. Since C is the third note in an A minor scale, the note C is called the third.) That note, the third, is what determines whether a scale or chord is major or minor. Last week we played an A major scale and arpeggio, so we played C♯s. This week we're practicing A minor, so we're using C♯s.

Tip: Go slowly and make sure your intonation is spot on. If you learn to be accurate you can learn to play fast, but if you're inaccurate your playing will always sound a little "off."

FRI

Workout #19   **Rhythm Track:** #2   **Technique:** Playing with Others   **Genre:** Rock/Pop

Description: Simple figures of constant, rhythmic eighth notes can be very potent in pop and rock music.

Tip: Play without vibrato and keep these notes rhythmic and precise. (If you're accidentally touching the open A string with your left hand, try bringing your elbow around under the violin to give your fingers more of a curve.) This example is played off the string near the frog. It's okay to have some grit in the sound!

SAT

Workout #20   **Rhythm Track:** #2   **Technique:** Bowing   **Genre:** Any pop style

Description: A big part of sounding "right" in pop music is getting the articulations down. Today we'll look at a basic bow stroke that's really useful.

Tip: Hold these notes out for their full value. Be conscious of beginning and ending the notes precisely in time. Don't taper the notes at all and end them rhythmically. Try releasing the pressure of your left-hand fingers at the end of each note.

SUN

Workout #21   **Rhythm Track:** #5   **Technique:** Stretching Out   **Genre:** Pop

About the Example: This exercise will introduce you to the sound of the Dorian scale. Put some separation on the eighth notes to keep this rhythmic.

MON

Workout #22   **Rhythm Track:** #3   **Technique:** Scales   **Genre:** Any

Description: The relationship between major and minor scales that we discussed last week is also true of pentatonic scales. Today we'll play an A minor pentatonic scale.

Tip: This A minor pentatonic scale uses the same pitches as the C major pentatonic scale but has a different sound. Pay attention to this relationship as you play the exercise. The minor pentatonic scale is hugely important in pop music. Add a few bends and you'll be able to develop a big vocabulary of licks and melodies!

TUE

Workout #23   **Rhythm Track:** #2   **Technique:** Ornaments   **Genre:** Any pop style

Description: Here come some funky grace notes!

Tip: Play the grace notes right on the beat, not as a pickup note. If you were tapping your foot, the grace note would occur right when your toe hits the floor. The second, regularly notated note should occur immediately after the beat.

WED

Workout #24   **Rhythm Track:** #4   **Technique:** Rhythm/Feel   **Genre:** Swing/Jazz

Description: Here's a good basic four-bar swing riff. It's notated with straight eighths, but the word "swing" at the beginning signals that it's up to the player to deliver a cool, swinging rhythm. Listen to the recording to get a sense of what that might sound like.

Tip: Keep repeating this passage, playing along with your metronome. Work to match the sound on the audio track. Make sure you don't rush! You don't need to play this the same way each time. Experiment with giving different notes more or less importance.

THU

Workout #25 **Rhythm Track:** #6 **Technique:** Arpeggios **Genre:** Any

Description: Let's take our major arpeggio from Week 1 and lower it a half step. Having to rely on the fourth finger for many of the notes can make playing in keys with several flats less comfortable on the violin, but these keys are common in jazz and when working with singers. Go slowly and work on building your strength and confidence with your pinkie.

Tip: To help your pinkie feel stronger and have more reach, make sure that you're not supporting the neck of the violin on your palm or wrist. It's tempting to support the violin that way, but it will slow you down and make things more difficult as you try to advance your playing.

FRI

Workout #26 **Rhythm Track:** #2 **Technique:** Playing with Others **Genre:** Rock/Pop

Description: This simple figure leaves plenty of space for someone to sing or play. When you're accompanying, it's important not to get in the way. Sparse, repetitive figures keep the focus on the person with the important line.

Tip: Bring out the pitches that change from measure to measure. Have a go at playing this exercise pizzicato as well. Like the etude in Week 2, try repeating this figure while a friend makes up a melody on the white keys of a piano.

SAT

Workout #27 **Rhythm Track:** #4 **Technique:** Bowing **Genre:** Swing/Jazz

Description: Here's a good exercise to develop more independence between your hands. This is the basic bowing of jazz and swing music. Because of the pattern of slurs, this bowing pattern is sometimes referred to as a "chain" bowing.

Tip: Practice this bowing starting both up-bow and down-bow. Use the printed fingering so that all the notes are on the same string. Begin by playing straight eighth notes, then add some swing to the rhythm, as demonstrated on the recording.

SUN

Workout #28 **Rhythm Track:** #5 **Technique:** Stretching Out **Genre:** Pop

About the Example: For this exercise we'll add some bends to an E minor pentatonic scale. Keep the bends small, around a quarter step.

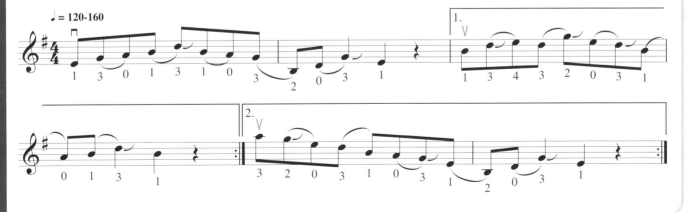

11

MON

Workout #29   **Rhythm Track:** #2   **Technique:** Scales   **Genre:** Any

Description: This exercise uses the notes of an A major scale to create an ascending pattern of thirds. A third is the interval, or distance, that's formed by skipping a note in a scale – A to C#, B to D, and so on. You can get more mileage out of any scale by applying a pattern like this to it.

Tip: Set your tuner to play a drone on the note A, and keep every note perfectly in tune. More advanced players can try playing this pattern in other keys.

TUE

Workout #30   **Rhythm Track:** #2   **Technique:** Ornaments   **Genre:** Any pop style

Description: Today we'll play a "chop" on the violin. This is a percussive technique that can expand the violin's roles in popular music. We'll use a downward arrow to indicate the bow stroke described below.

Tip: Roll the bow in your fingers so that the hair is facing away from you and bring the bow down at a slight angle toward the fingerboard. Instead of using an up- or down-bow, land vertically from above and leave the bow on the string. Lightly dampen the strings with your left hand. The placement of your fingers doesn't matter. You just want a percussive sound without a distinct pitch.

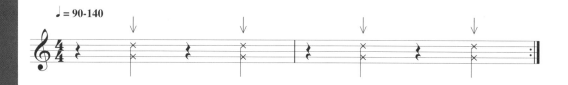

WED

Workout #31   **Rhythm Track:** #4   **Technique:** Rhythm/Feel   **Genre:** Swing/Jazz

Description: Now let's add some syncopation to our swing vocabulary. Listen to the recording to get a better understanding of the rhythm.

Tip: Stay relaxed when you play these rhythms and make sure not to rush ahead of your metronome. Once you're comfortable, try experimenting with different bowings.

THU

Workout #32   **Rhythm Track:** #2   **Technique:** Arpeggios   **Genre:** Any

Description: This week let's play an Amin7 arpeggio. You can form a minor 7th chord by playing the first, third, fifth, and seventh notes of a natural minor scale or a Dorian scale. We'll play up – then down – over two octaves, then rearrange the same pitches into a different order to get more comfortable with them.

Tip: Once you're comfortable with this exercise, play it a whole step higher, beginning on the note B. If that's easy for you to do, try some more keys until you've played all 12 possible minor 7th chords.

FRI

Workout #33   **Rhythm Track:** #5   **Technique:** Playing with Others   **Genre:** Rock/Roots

Description: Bo Diddley was a blues and early rock guitarist and singer. Let's play a simple but effective riff with an underlying Bo Diddley rhythm. The rhythm made by the accented notes in this exercise was a signature of his.

Tip: The rhythm should be a kind of lazy, almost straight-eighth-note feel. Check out the recording. Once you've got the notes in your fingers, concentrate on getting a good feel with the rhythm and accents. The unaccented notes can be played very lightly.

SAT

Workout #34   **Rhythm Track:** #4   **Technique:** Bowing   **Genre:** Swing/Jazz

Description: Let's start swinging with moving notes in the left hand and our "chain" bowing in the right. Use the open E string where it's marked. For now we'll practice slurs without a string crossing.

Tip: Practice this exercise with straight-eighth notes first, then add some swing. Keep focusing on the rhythm of the eighth notes. Use a smooth, horizontal bow stroke. Because you're slurring every other note, much of the rhythm is going to come from your left hand.

SUN

Workout #35   **Rhythm Track:** #2   **Technique:** Stretching Out   **Genre:** Pop

About the Example: Good pop music tends to combine a number of simple ideas into something interesting. With just a basic blues scale, some bends, and some grace notes, you can generate a melody like this.

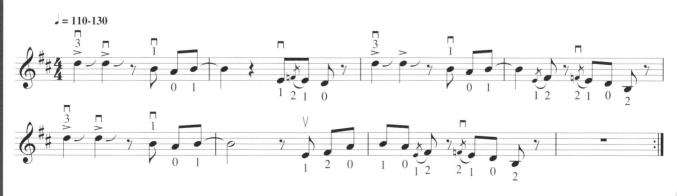

MON

Workout #36 **Rhythm Track:** #5 **Technique:** Scales **Genre:** Any

Description: As a violinist, it's common to learn the natural minor scale, but a more useful minor scale for pop music is the Dorian scale. It raises the sixth note of the minor scale by a half step and produces a hipper, more modern sound when used in a tune. (The pattern of this scale is identical to that of a major scale begun on its second note, or from D to D on the white keys of the piano.)

Tip: Pay attention to the pattern of intervals that produce this scale and its sound. When you're able to, play this scale starting on other pitches. Soon you should be able to play it in different keys without thinking about every note.

TUE

Workout #37 **Rhythm Track:** #2 **Technique:** Ornaments **Genre:** Any pop style

Description: Now let's add an up-stroke to our chop repertoire. We'll use an upward arrow to indicate the bow stroke described below.

Tip: Roll the bow in your fingers so that the hair is facing away from you. Start the stroke with the bow on the string and play a short up-bow that immediately comes off the string. Dampen the strings lightly with your left hand – what fingers you use and their exact placement doesn't matter – so that you make a short, percussive sound without a distinct pitch.

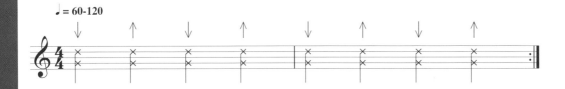

WED

Workout #38 **Rhythm Track:** #4 **Technique:** Rhythm/Feel **Genre:** Swing/Jazz

Description: Let's add another layer of syncopation to our swing practice. The recording will help you figure out this rhythm.

Tip: There are lots of ways to swing and the exact rhythms are always subtly changing. Instead of thinking of swing as a specific rhythm or subdivision, listen to as many players as you can and incorporate into your playing the feels and rhythms that get you excited.

THU

Workout #39 **Rhythm Track:** #5 **Technique:** Arpeggios **Genre:** Any

Description: This week we'll continue playing arpeggios of 7th chords, which are common in popular music. A 7th chord simply stacks one more third onto the basic triad that we've been studying. We'll begin with the major 7th chord. This chord is constructed by playing every other note (the first, third, fifth, and seventh note) of a major scale.

Tip: In the second half of the exercise, when you have pairs of notes that use the same finger on adjacent strings, try putting your finger down on both strings at once. This will make your playing much more efficient.

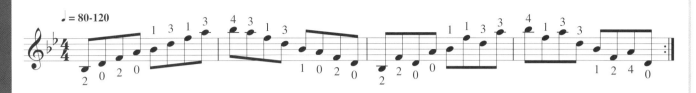

FRI

Workout #40 **Rhythm Track:** #2 **Technique:** Playing with Others **Genre:** Latin

Description: This is a version of a standard Latin riff. If you like this, you might want to check out some Latin dance music. There are many subgenres, but searching out some salsa music might turn up sounds you'll enjoy.

Tip: Play these notes very rhythmically. Each note is sustained, but with an abrupt end, right at the following rest.

SAT

Workout #41 **Rhythm Track:** #4 **Technique:** Bowing **Genre:** Swing/Jazz

Description: Here's our chain bowing with what is sometimes referred to as the bebop scale. (Bebop is a jazz style that is best personified by saxophonist Charlie Parker. You should check him out!) The point of this exercise is to get some practice with this bowing while moving around the fingerboard with the left hand.

Tip: The printed fingering leaves out any slurred string crossings for now. If you'd like to try adding them in, just reverse the open string and fourth finger markings.

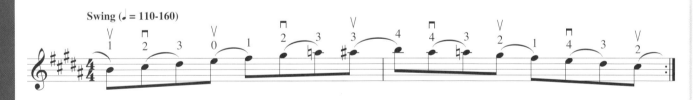

SUN

Workout #42 **Rhythm Track:** #2 **Technique:** Stretching Out **Genre:** Latin

About the Example: Here's a Latin-tinged melody in A major with a two-bar introduction. The double stops all use an open string.

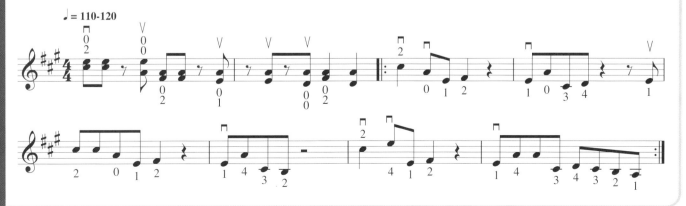

15

MON

Workout #43   **Rhythm Track:** #2   **Technique:** Scales   **Genre:** Any

Description: The chromatic scale moves by half steps through all 12 notes. If you're not yet familiar with all the notes in first position, use this exercise to find them.

Tip: If you're just getting comfortable with this scale, use the bottom fingering. If this is a familiar scale, use the top fingering and push yourself to go faster. You can also play the scale backward (descending) if you're looking for a more rigorous workout.

TUE

Workout #44   **Rhythm Track:** #2   **Technique:** Ornaments   **Genre:** Any pop style

Description: Let's combine our up- and down-bow chops from Weeks 5 and 6. Remember to roll the bow in your fingers so that the hair is facing away from you. Darol Anger is a master of the chop and has used it on a lot of recordings. You definitely should check him out.

Tip: Make sure to leave the bow firmly on the string at the end of the down chop so that it's ready for the up chop. Use the fingers of your left hand to lightly stop the strings. We're going for a percussive sound with no real pitch.

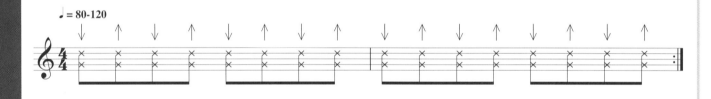

WED

Workout #45   **Rhythm Track:** #4   **Technique:** Rhythm/Feel   **Genre:** Swing/Jazz

Description: Let's add some accents and rests into the mix. Keep swinging! You might want to listen to Svend Asmussen for inspiration.

Tip: Play the accented notes strongly and let the other notes be less important. (They're there less as part of the melodic figure and more as a rhythmic feel.) Pick a pitch and make up some swing rhythms of your own. You don't need to play anything complicated. Simple, repetitive rhythmic figures can be powerful.

THU

Workout #46   **Rhythm Track:** #2   **Technique:** Arpeggios   **Genre:** Any

Description: Let's play an arpeggio on a minor 7th chord. A minor 7th chord can be broken down into two fifths: one between the root and fifth, and one between the third and seventh. Because the violin is tuned in fifths, it's a useful way to think of this chord. These relationships are evident in bar 3.

Tip: Because fifths are played with one finger across two strings, intonation can be difficult. When possible, play both pitches without hopping your finger from one note to the other. Instead, aim for the fingerboard in between the strings. If you need to fix the intonation, lean your hand slightly to the right or left to effect small variations in pitch.

FRI

Workout #47   **Rhythm Track:** #5   **Technique:** Playing with Others   **Genre:** Rock

Description: This is a standard boogie-woogie or early rock riff. It's a figure that's often played on guitar or piano.

Tip: Play these notes off the string with a driving rhythm. It's just fine to be a little gritty!

SAT

Workout #48   **Rhythm Track:** #5   **Technique:** Bowing   **Genre:** Any

Description: Let's add some string crossings to our slurs. The timing of the string crossing will feel a little different depending on whether it's on an up-bow or down-bow.

Tip: Put a rest in between the two-note slurs to isolate each string crossing. Once you're comfortable, play the exercise as written. You want to keep the rhythm absolutely steady whether you're playing an up- or a down-bow. Feeling an accent on each beat may help.

SUN

Workout #49   **Rhythm Track:** #4   **Technique:** Stretching Out   **Genre:** Swing/Jazz

About the Example: Today we'll practice swinging with a bluesy figure over an E7 chord.

MON

Workout #50   **Rhythm Track:** #2   **Technique:** Scales   **Genre:** Any

Description: This is a great exercise to improve your intonation and build a good hand frame. Sustain through each note and connect it to the next as much as possible.

Tip: Keep your finger down on the first note of each pair as you play the second note, like a double stop. Use your pinkie instead of the open strings. Practice this slowly and use a drone on A to highlight any inaccuracies.

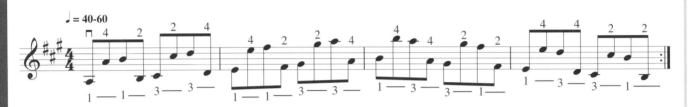

TUE

Workout #51   **Rhythm Track:** #2   **Technique:** Ornaments   **Genre:** Any pop style

Description: Let's use a stroke that allows you to add some pitched notes to your chop.

Tip: Start the stroke with your bow firmly on the string, right next to the frog. Make a quick, short up-bow that immediately comes off the strings. Keep your left-hand fingers down firmly so that the pitches can ring.

WED

Workout #52   **Rhythm Track:** #7   **Technique:** Rhythm/Feel   **Genre:** Bluegrass

Description: Here's a chance to work on your fiddle tune feel. This passage is all on the A string. With no string crossings to worry about, you can focus on the rhythm and feel.

Tip: Play these eighth notes straight, then add a tiny bit of swing. That can really bring this style to life. The swinging rhythm and feel can be subtle and is a little different than in jazz, but the best fiddle players often inject a swinging, rhythmic lilt into their playing. Check out Byron Berline!

THU

Workout #53   **Rhythm Track:** #6   **Technique:** Arpeggios   **Genre:** Any

Description: Let's go a little farther with the fourth finger extension we worked on in Week 2. There will be passages that will be much easier to play if you're comfortable using that same pinkie stretch on the lower strings. We'll use B major to introduce this idea.

Tip: Remember to keep your left wrist relaxed and roughly straight. It will help to think of your third and fourth fingers as a unit. When you reach for the D♯ on the G string, putting those two fingers down together will help your pinkie feel stronger.

FRI

Workout #54   **Rhythm Track:** #5   **Technique:** Playing with Others   **Genre:** Country

Description: If you're asked to kick off a country tune in the key of D, you might play something like this.

Tip: Begin by playing only the lower notes; they're all on the D string. Then add your open A. Start with your bow above the string for the first three notes. Make the pickup notes short with strong accents; the bow should come off the string immediately. The rest of the exercise uses smooth, long bows.

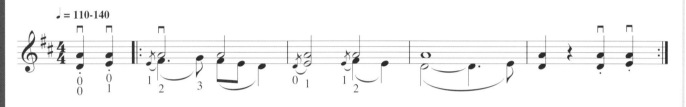

SAT

Workout #55   **Rhythm Track:** #5   **Technique:** Bowing   **Genre:** Any

Description: This exercise will increase your bowing independence as you get more comfortable with the string crossings we began developing last week.

Tip: Crossing strings while slurring tends to be the challenging part of this technique. It's difficult at first to change strings without changing direction. Start slowly. If you're having trouble getting this going, review the examples from Weeks 5 and 6.

SUN

Workout #56   **Rhythm Track:** #2   **Technique:** Stretching Out   **Genre:** Rock/Funk

About the Example: Here's a funk-rock lick to work with. Keep your bowing rhythmic and punchy.

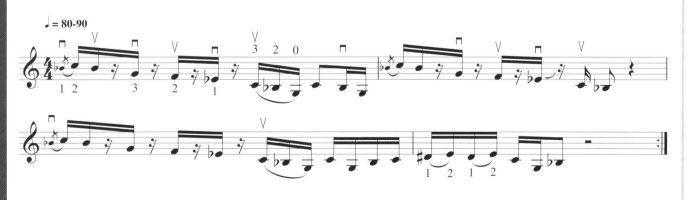

19

MON

Workout #57 **Rhythm Track:** #3 **Technique:** Scales **Genre:** Any

Description: This basic blues scale is identical to the minor pentatonic scale, but with one added note: the ♭5. You can play other pitches in the blues, obviously, but these are good go-to notes if you're getting your feet wet with improvising.

Tip: The scale as written works well for minor-key blues tunes. To use it in a major key, play an upward pitch bend on the third (B♭, in this case). Improvise some licks or melodies using these notes. You don't need to be fancy; pick two or three notes to use. That's all you need to come up with tons of really cool licks.

TUE

Workout #58 **Rhythm Track:** #2 **Technique:** Ornaments **Genre:** Any pop style

Description: Here's a funky lick that will keep your left hand busy.

Tip: Follow the printed fingering. Start practicing by playing each pair of grace and eighth notes slowly. Once you're comfortable, play the whole exercise and start raising the tempo.

WED

Workout #59 **Rhythm Track:** #5 **Technique:** Rhythm/Feel **Genre:** Latin

Description: A clave (pronounced "KLAH-vay") is a percussion instrument (one of a pair of thick wooden dowels that are struck together), but it's also a rhythmic pattern. The first two bars of the exercise are the basic clave rhythm; the next two bars are sometimes referred to as a reverse clave.

Tip: With this pizzicato passage we're trying to emulate the sound of claves, the instrument. These notes are resonant but very short. If you're not familiar with this instrument, find a recording. You'll almost certainly recognize the sound.

THU

Workout #60   **Rhythm Track:** #3   **Technique:** Arpeggios   **Genre:** Any

Description: G major is an excellent key for beginning to play double stops that don't use an open string. These aren't truly chords – chords have three or more notes – but they can serve that sort of function on the violin.

Tip: Start by playing one note from each pair before adding in the second. Go slowly and work to play perfectly in tune. If you're using a drone to check your intonation, make sure your G string is in tune. If you're tuning the violin to itself from an A, it's easy to have the fifths get too wide and make your G string too low.

FRI

Workout #61   **Rhythm Track:** #2   **Technique:** Playing with Others   **Genre:** Pop

Description: Pizzicato can get overlooked as a musical device. Here's a generic riff that might be used in a pop song.

Tip: This will work in playing position, but you might get more volume and authority from playing in "guitar position" and plucking everything with your thumb.

SAT

Workout #62   **Rhythm Track:** #2   **Technique:** Bowing   **Genre:** Rock/Funk

Description: This excerpt takes our concept from Weeks 2 and 3 a little further. Today we'll fancy up the bowing and add a little melody.

Tip: Keep the same things in mind as before. Subdivide the beat in your head. Sustain your sound throughout each note and put a distinct ending precisely on the next rest.

SUN

Workout #63   **Rhythm Track:** #5   **Technique:** Stretching Out   **Genre:** Country

About the Example: This country shuffle begins with two short, accented double stops on beats 3 and 4. This sort of figure is a standard kick-off for country songs.

MON

Workout #64   Rhythm Track: #5   Technique: Scales   Genre: Any

Description: Today we'll be working with the melodic minor scale. In classical pedagogy, the melodic minor is often played as two different scales, one to ascend, the other when descending. The descending scale is just the natural minor that we've already looked at. It's the ascending melodic minor scale that we're interested in. That's the scale that's being referred to in popular music.

Tip: The melodic minor scale is a natural minor scale with its sixth and seventh degrees raised by a half step. It is also identical to a major scale with a ♭3rd. We're using G as the root.

TUE

Workout #65   Rhythm Track: #2   Technique: Ornaments   Genre: Any pop style

Description: Let's put our pitched up-bow chop from Week 8 together with our down chop.

Tip: You might feel uncoordinated when you first try this. Go slowly until the motions become comfortable. Casey Driessen is a chop wizard you definitely should check out.

WED

Workout #66   Rhythm Track: #2   Technique: Rhythm/Feel   Genre: Any pop style

Description: Today we'll be developing a bow stroke that allows you to add unpitched rhythms to a figure. Listen to the recording to get a sense of what you're going for.

Tip: These aren't chops. Instead, play near the frog and use a vertical stroke that begins above, and immediately comes off, the string. With your left hand, dampen the strings so that you don't hear a specific pitch. The fingers you use and their placement don't matter. This is the sort of thing you can add to a passage to make it more interesting and powerful.

THU

Workout #67   **Rhythm Track:** #5   **Technique:** Arpeggios   **Genre:** Any

Description: Today's exercise arpeggiates a Gm(maj7) chord. This chord can be formed by playing every other note of the melodic minor scale. It's a colorful sonority that has a film-noir, private-eye characteristic.

Tip: Be aware of the diagonal hop that your finger has to make to go from the ♭3 of B♭ to the maj7 of F♯. Make sure your pitch is good and that the F♯ is high enough.

FRI

Workout #68   **Rhythm Track:** #2   **Technique:** Playing with Others   **Genre:** Any pop style

Description: The opening bar of this exercise is there just to help get the sound of G major in your ear. The four bars that follow are a take on a standard figure that alternates between a G7 and G7sus chord. ("Sus" is the abbreviation for a suspension, a note in a chord that feels the need to resolve to a chord tone next door.)

Tip: To tune a perfect fifth on the violin, you can lean your hand slightly to the left or right. This will alter the pitches by slightly changing the shape of your fingertips as they press down.

SAT

Workout #69   **Rhythm Track:** #2   **Technique:** Bowing   **Genre:** Pop/Funk

Description: Let's go farther with the bow stroke we've been working on. We're going to play it as a rapid series of bows in the same direction. It's not too tricky and it naturally gives a cool articulation to the notes. The first two eighths of each group should sound like 16ths with 16th rests.

Tip: Remember to release the pressure at the end of each note, just before you stop the bow. Then put pressure back into the bow before starting the next note. Check out the recording if you're unsure of the sound you're going for.

SUN

Workout #70   **Rhythm Track:** #4   **Technique:** Stretching Out   **Genre:** Swing/Jazz

About the Example: Here's an exercise that combines two swing riffs in C. Try practicing this with your metronome playing on beats 2 and 4.

MON

Workout #71   **Rhythm Track:** #5   **Technique:** Scales   **Genre:** Any

Description: Today we'll play a C Mixolydian scale. Mixolydian is the basic scale that works with a dominant chord. Chords referred to with a note name followed by just a "7," like A7, A♭7 and E7, are dominant chords. We'll learn more about dominant chords later in the book. For now, just get the sound of this scale in your ear. You'll use it a lot.

Tip: A Mixolydian scale is identical to a major scale except that the last note (the seventh) is a half step lower. In a C major scale, the seventh note is B. In a C Mixolydian scale, the seventh note is B♭.

TUE

Workout #72   **Rhythm Track:** #4   **Technique:** Ornaments   **Genre:** Any pop style

Description: Ghost notes are quiet tones that can add rhythm and interest to a figure you're playing. They can be a quiet note with your regular tone or have a raspy, rhythmic tone. They don't need to have a beautiful sound, they just need to feel good. Let's play some!

Tip: Make the up-bow, ghosted notes very quiet. You can skate the bow over the string instead of putting any weight into it with your arm. Listen to the recording to get a better idea of this. Start slowly and make a big contrast between the regular and ghosted notes.

WED

Workout #73   **Rhythm Track:** #2   **Technique:** Rhythm/Feel   **Genre:** Pop

Description: The point of this exercise is to set up a sparse, rhythmic figure that leaves plenty of space for other instruments, but that is groovy all on its own.

Tip: After the initial, quick chords you'll have to be patient not to play the chops on beats 2 and 4 too soon. Focus on your metronome and subdivide in your head.

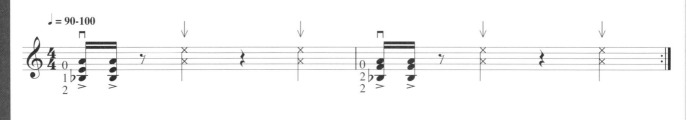

THU

Workout #74   **Rhythm Track:** #3   **Technique:** Arpeggios   **Genre:** Any

Description: An important part of being versatile in pop music is being able to play double stops. It helps you to accompany people and to play a role in the band other than just playing fills or melodies. Today we're in the key of A. We'll be using the same notes as our A arpeggio from Week 1, but we'll play pairs of those notes at the same time.

Tip: It's important to play these in tune. Go slowly and tune each double stop. You might want to begin by playing one note from each pair and then adding its harmony note once you're sure about your intonation.

FRI

Workout #75   **Rhythm Track:** #4   **Technique:** Playing with Others   **Genre:** Swing/Jazz

Description: Don't forget how much dynamic interest the violin can have. This figure is something like what a horn section might repeat as a background behind a soloist.

Tip: Make the sforzandos and crescendos dramatic. Use your whole bow and create as much excitement as you can!

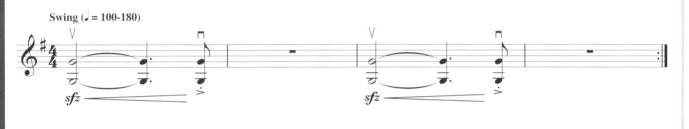

SAT

Workout #76   **Rhythm Track:** #4   **Technique:** Bowing   **Genre:** Swing/Jazz

Description: This exercise will continue building your ability to swing. This exercise highlights slurred string crossings in both directions. We're picking up where we left off in Week 8.

Tip: Practice this slowly until the rhythms and string crossings feel and sound good, then increase the tempo. Your rhythm is the most important part of this exercise.

SUN

Workout #77   **Rhythm Track:** #5   **Technique:** Stretching Out   **Genre:** Rock/Funk

About the Example: Use an aggressive, off-the-string bowing to bring this lick to life. Put some separation between the notes to keep this acutely rhythmic.

MON

Workout #78   **Rhythm Track:** #3   **Technique:** Scales   **Genre:** Any

Description: This is a more complete version of the blues scale introduced in Week 9. It's like an A major scale that also includes the ♭3, the ♭5, and the ♭7. The blues scale isn't just for blues songs. The blues vocabulary is a part of most popular music styles.

Tip: Once you're comfortable, slide between the neighboring half-steps of the third, fifth, and seventh. If you can get comfortable with those notes and the microtones in between them, a whole new world of expression will open up for you. You should also play this exercise backward, as a descending blues scale.

TUE

Workout #79   **Rhythm Track:** #4   **Technique:** Ornaments   **Genre:** Any pop style

Description: Let's practice our ghost notes by playing a repeating four-note pattern and making it feel good. The ghost notes can be a quiet open D string or they can sound more like a rhythmic noise or harmonic by lightly skating the bow across the string.

Tip: You want a big dynamic contrast between the regular notes and the ghosted ones. Practice releasing the weight of your right arm for the ghost notes. For a more raspy sound, release your third finger just enough to dampen the string.

WED

Workout #80   **Rhythm Track:** #5   **Technique:** Rhythm/Feel   **Genre:** Rock/Roots

Description: Here's another take on the Bo Diddley rhythm. This figure – played with a shuffle-y, barely swung rhythm – is named for the legendary guitarist and singer, who also played some violin! It is basically the clave rhythm we studied in Week 9, but played with a swingy lilt.

Tip: Listen to the recording for an example of this rhythm. You may want to start by practicing it with a straight-eighth rhythm, then giving it just a slight bit of swing. Be sure to listen to Bo Diddley!

THU

Workout #81   **Rhythm Track:** #5   **Technique:** Arpeggios   **Genre:** Any

Description: Here's another dominant-chord arpeggio, this time a D7.

Tip: Pay attention to the intonation of the notes you're playing with your second finger on the D and A strings. Extra attention is sometimes needed to make sure those notes are in tune as you switch between a "high" and "low" second finger. Keep your third finger down as you reach up for the C on the E string.

FRI

Workout #82   **Rhythm Track:** #4   **Technique:** Playing with Others   **Genre:** Blues

Description: This is a blues cliché that you can get a lot of mileage out of.

Tip: Bring out the pitched figure at the beginning, then keep the chops in the background to allow a singer or soloist to shine. Feel free to spontaneously declare who done you wrong and describe some of the ways your luck has been bad.

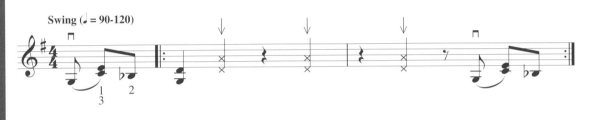

SAT

Workout #83   **Rhythm Track:** #4   **Technique:** Bowing   **Genre:** Swing/Jazz

Description: Here's a lick that combines a number of the bowing components we've learned so far.

Tip: If you're having trouble with this, isolate the problem area. Make a repeating loop of the tricky notes and repeat it until it feels better. You can also review the exercises we've done that focus on the technique you're struggling with.

SUN

Workout #84   **Rhythm Track:** #1   **Technique:** Stretching Out   **Genre:** Pop

About the Example: Here's a little tune with a time signature that alternates between 4/4 and 3/4. Listen to the recording and you'll easily get it going.

MON

Workout #85   **Rhythm Track:** #2   **Technique:** Scales   **Genre:** Any
Description: This exercise expands on our skills from Week 8 and adds the difficulty of a key with a number of flats. The goal is to keep your finger down on the first note of each pair while playing the lower octave. This will help build an excellent hand frame.
Tip: Go slowly and keep your intonation as perfect as possible. Keep an A♭ drone in the background. Instead of simply reaching for pitches with your fingers, use your left elbow to bring the fingers of your left hand where they need to be.

TUE

Workout #86   **Rhythm Track:** #4   **Technique:** Ornaments   **Genre:** Any pop style
Description: Let's try another ghost note exercise with a more complex pattern. Listen to the recording to better understand what you're going for.
Tip: The ghosted notes should be subtle and kept in the background. Take the weight out of the bow on the ghost notes and let the bow slide across the strings without much pressure. This will give you a good feel with subtle ghost notes. Experiment with lightening the pressure in your left hand on the ghost notes to get a different timbre.

WED

Workout #87   **Rhythm Track:** #4   **Technique:** Rhythm/Feel   **Genre:** Swing/Jazz
Description: This is a simple, common swing rhythm. It's easy to read, but you want to work to get it feeling right.
Tip: Experiment with accenting different notes of the pattern. Keeping the second note of each pair short helps this rhythm to feel "right."

THU

Workout #88   **Rhythm Track:** #6   **Technique:** Arpeggios   **Genre:** Any

Description: This week we'll play a D minor arpeggio and go a little higher up the neck. To play the second and third groups of three notes, we'll need to shift to third position. (This is called "third position" because your first finger is going where your third finger normally would. If you put your first finger where your pinkie normally goes, you're in fourth position, and so on.)

Tip: Make sure to keep your hand frame consistent and move your whole hand up. Keep your pinkie roughly above the string, even if you're not playing a note with it.

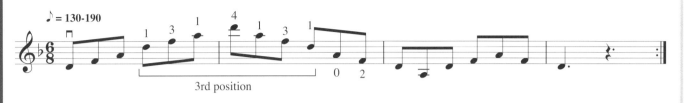

FRI

Workout #89   **Rhythm Track:** #4   **Technique:** Playing with Others   **Genre:** Swing/Jazz

Description: We can use little rhythmic accents on the "ands," the second eighth note of each beat, to create more rhythmic interest.

Tip: The quarter-note pulses are still the fundamental part of the figure. The eighth notes should function like ornaments to the following downbeat note. The figure begins up-bow so that the down-bow helps bring out the accents. Some separation between the quarter notes can help the feel on a figure like this. Release the pressure in your left hand as you slow the bow.

SAT

Workout #90   **Rhythm Track:** #7   **Technique:** Bowing   **Genre:** Bluegrass

Description: This is the basic shuffle rhythm in the right hand that permeates so much fiddle music. The left hand moves during the slur to create a constant eighth-note pattern. These two concepts, put together, form the basic underlying pattern of tons of fiddle playing. This exercise is really worth perfecting!

Tip: Practice this exercise with straight-eighth notes first, then add just a hint of swing. Fiddle music often has a subtler swing than jazz does. It's just the hint of a lilt that can make fiddle tunes really come alive.

SUN

Workout #91   **Rhythm Track:** #7   **Technique:** Stretching Out   **Genre:** Cajun/Bluegrass

About the Example: This exercise looks tricky, but all the double stops use an open string. You can play this smoothly or with a little separation for a different feel.

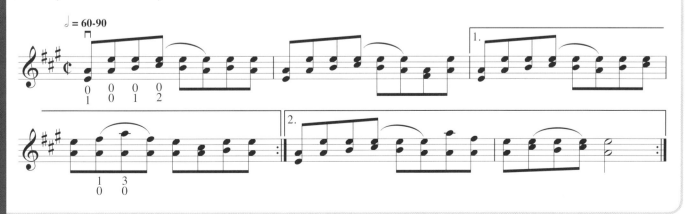

MON

Workout #92   **Rhythm Track:** #5   **Technique:** Scales   **Genre:** Any

Description: To get more comfortable with the Mixolydian scale, we'll play it as a pattern of triads. Practicing a sequence derived from a scale is a great way to become more comfortable with that scale. Scales played as a sequence often feel different than when they're played stepwise.

Tip: Because the notes of A Mixolydian are the same as those of D major, it's easy to have your ear pulled toward D. Use a drone on A to keep your mind planted in the right key. Sequences like this can be used with any scale.

TUE

Workout #93   **Rhythm Track:** #4   **Technique:** Ornaments   **Genre:** Any pop style

Description: This exercise puts a ghost note at the end of a slur. The regular note (E, in this case) should be much more prominent than the ghosted note. It's important for the ghost note to be much quieter than the "regular" notes, but the quality of the note is up to you. It can be a quiet pitched note, sometimes referred to as a "swallowed" note, or just a rhythmic noise.

Tip: Take the pressure out of the bow on the second note of each slur so that it's almost hidden. You can play either a quiet pitched note or lift your left-hand fingers off the fingerboard just enough to blur the pitch.

WED

Workout #94   **Rhythm Track:** #5   **Technique:** Rhythm/Feel   **Genre:** Rock/Roots

Description: Here is our Bo Diddley rhythm from Week 12, but with the addition of an underlying eighth-note groove.

Tip: First, practice this as a straight-eighth figure, then give it a slightly swung lilt for a looser feel. You don't need to be precise about the double stops. It's fine to have some open Ds on the unaccented notes.

THU

Workout #95   **Rhythm Track:** #6   **Technique:** Arpeggios   **Genre:** Any

Description: Let's go just a little higher up the neck with an E major arpeggio. Learning to shift is beyond the scope of this book, but there are many books and videos available to help you get started.

Tip: This week you'll need to shift to fourth position. Your first finger will be where your pinkie normally goes. When you shift up, move your entire hand – rather than reaching with a single finger – so that your pinkie is ready to play and can drop straight down onto the fingerboard.

FRI

Workout #96   **Rhythm Track:** #2   **Technique:** Playing with Others   **Genre:** Pop/Rock

Description: If you're looking for something to play as part of a group, you can always outline the chords with double stops like the ones we've worked on. You don't need to understand the chord symbols printed above the music in order to play this exercise. The symbols shown here are ones like you might see in a part or write yourself in order to tell other musicians what to play.

Tip: A lick like this would work in a pop song. Play this without vibrato and be very rhythmic.

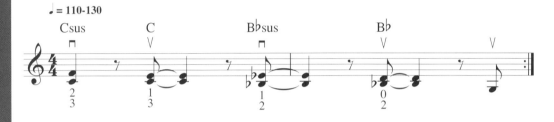

SAT

Workout #97   **Rhythm Track:** #7   **Technique:** Bowing   **Genre:** Bluegrass

Description: This exercise builds on last week's and adds more movement for the left hand.

Tip: This figure epitomizes the basic approach to fiddle tunes. Practice the pattern until it's second nature. As you progress and add more components to this basic framework, the time you put in will pay off.

SUN

Workout #98   **Rhythm Track:** #5   **Technique:** Stretching Out   **Genre:** Irish

About the Example: Here's a joyous jig to complete your weekend!

MON

Workout #99 **Rhythm Track:** #5 **Technique:** Scales **Genre:** Any

Description: If you raise the fourth note of the major scale by a half step, you have the Lydian scale. This scale is derived from the major scale and is the pattern of intervals created by starting on the major scale's fourth note.

Tip: This scale can work well with major and major 7th chords. It turns a somewhat dissonant note (E♭, in this case) into a more consonant pitch (E♮). Also, it just sounds cool. Interestingly, this is a not uncommon scale to hear in a fiddle tune. If you'd like, practice it with a little rhythmic lilt, as in a fiddle tune.

TUE

Workout #100 **Rhythm Track:** #2 **Technique:** Ornaments **Genre:** Any pop style

Description: Today we'll play a slide up to a note.

Tip: The slide up is very quick and begins right on the beat. Hold the quarter note for its full value without dissipating the sound. End the note abruptly on the next beat. Listen to the recording to hear the sound you're after.

WED

Workout #101 **Rhythm Track:** #5 **Technique:** Rhythm/Feel **Genre:** Blues/Swing

Description: Here's a swing lick with a tricky looking first beat. If you check out the recording, it will seem less confusing. Now and then violinists will play a quick ornament like this between two more important notes.

Tip: These notes go by quickly and are sometimes chosen for their comfort on the instrument. When you dissect a lick like this from your favorite player, you may find that it doesn't sound great slowed down – but, as a quick flourish, gestures like this can be flashy and exciting!

THU

Workout #102   **Rhythm Track:** #5   **Technique:** Arpeggios   **Genre:** Any

Description: Today we'll play double stops that outline a major chord and go a little higher up the fingerboard. This week we're playing in D major and will need to shift up to third position.

Tip: If you're not comfortable with third position yet, play the lower note of the high double-stops. There's still plenty here for you to work on. If playing both notes at once is tricky, play them one at a time, the lower note and then the higher one, as eighth notes.

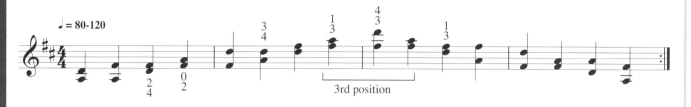

FRI

Workout #103   **Rhythm Track:** #2   **Technique:** Playing with Others   **Genre:** Latin/Pop

Description: You can create a background figure by using the thirds you've been practicing. This is something you might employ on a i-IV vamp in D minor. (In music, Roman numerals are used to denote chords. Lower-case numerals are minor chords; upper case indicates a major chord. In this D minor example, i is a D minor chord and IV is a G major chord.)

Tip: Play these eighth notes on the string, but with plenty of separation to help give them a little rhythmic drive. This passage could work well in a Latin tune.

SAT

Workout #104   **Rhythm Track:** #2   **Technique:** Bowing   **Genre:** Any pop style

Description: Pop music is full of musical figures that seem simple and straightforward, but actually have little touches that make them sound cool. The ends of notes often have a rhythmic component to them that isn't a part of classical music. This exercise will introduce this idea and give you some practice with it.

Tip: These quarter notes should be sustained and end distinctly on the next beat. Don't play a new note on the 16th, just end the long note abruptly and keep your bow on the string. If there's a tiny crunch, that's fine.

SUN

Workout #105   **Rhythm Track:** #2   **Technique:** Stretching Out   **Genre:** Latin/Pop

About the Example: This short, Latin-tinged tune will give you some practice with double stops and pop articulations.

WEEK 16

MON

Workout #106   **Rhythm Track:** #5   **Technique:** Scales   **Genre:** Any

Description: The keys that are most comfortable on the violin make a lot of use of the open strings. It can be tricky to play a tune in A♭ instead of A. Guitarists tend to use box shapes that they can move up and down the neck without hassle. Let's apply this concept to the violin.

Tip: This is the blues scale in G♭. (Not the violin's friendliest key!) If today's exercise feels tricky, review the first half of our blues scale exercise from Week 12, then try this one again. Play the example in third position. By moving your first finger to different starting notes and using the same pattern, you can easily play in what is normally a rather difficult key.

TUE

Workout #107   **Rhythm Track:** #4   **Technique:** Ornaments   **Genre:** Any pop style

Description: Let's practice some percussive down-bows that work like our pitched up-bow chops. We'll be playing down-bow figures that sound like the up-bows we learned in Week 8.

Tip: Start the pitched stroke with the bow firmly on the string. Play a short, quick down-bow that immediately comes off the strings and allows them to ring. You can also practice this exercise with a swing feel.

WED

Workout #108   **Rhythm Track:** #2   **Technique:** Rhythm/Feel   **Genre:** Any

Description: This exercise is a challenge because the accented, moving, syncopated notes draw your ear. It's difficult not to have these notes drift onto the beat.

Tip: Stick to your guns! Feel the rhythm of the down-bows even though they're unaccented. Keep concentrating on the sound of the click so you're not led astray.

THU

Workout #109 **Rhythm Track:** #5 **Technique:** Arpeggios **Genre:** Any

Description: Here's another major 7th chord, today on E♭. The exercise begins on the third of the chord so that you have a chance to play all the notes that are available in first position.

Tip: Do your best to play the fifths in the last bar without hopping your finger from string to string. Aim for the fingerboard between the notes and use the fleshy part of your finger without collapsing your knuckle.

FRI

Workout #110 **Rhythm Track:** #4 **Technique:** Playing with Others **Genre:** Jazz/Swing

Description: Here's a little vamp to work on your jazz feel. The letters above the notes are chord symbols. (Understanding them isn't necessary to play the exercise.) The "m7" after a note name means this is a minor 7th chord like we played in Week 5. The "7" is the dominant chord we've been exploring (Week 12), and "maj7" is the major 7th chord we worked with in Week 6.

Tip: Put a little separation between each note. Play this repeatedly as a continuous loop and work on keeping it groovy.

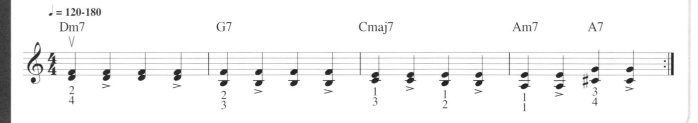

SAT

Workout #111 **Rhythm Track:** #2 **Technique:** Bowing **Genre:** Any pop style

Description: This exercise presents a very vertical, off-the-string bowing and is good practice to develop a short, rhythmic articulation that works well in a lot of pop music. Many instruments in pop music are percussive (drums, a plucked bass, piano, guitar) and horn players often use a sharp, tongued attack.

Tip: The key to making the violin fit in a lot of pop styles is being able to mimic that percussive attack. It takes practice, but don't feel cheated. Many guitarists' highest praise for a sustained, overdriven rock guitar sound is to describe it as violin-like.

SUN

Workout #112 **Rhythm Track:** #5 **Technique:** Stretching Out **Genre:** Blues/Pop

About the Example: This passage is played in third position except for bar 7, which is in second position. The double stop in bar 4 is played with your fourth finger in third position, along with the open A string.

MON

Workout #113 **Rhythm Track:** #2 **Technique:** Scales **Genre:** Any

Description: An excellent way to become more comfortable with the sound of a new scale is to play its notes in different patterns. By playing a sequence – a melodic shape that is repeated beginning on a different pitch – you're forced to solve puzzles regarding what notes go where.

Tip: This exercise is basically the A Dorian scale played in fourths. For scales derived from the major scale, including this one, all the fourths will be perfect fourths (five half steps), with one exception – the augmented fourth (tritone; six half steps). If you can internalize this, you'll be able to understand these scales intellectually in addition to being able to play them by ear.

TUE

Workout #114 **Rhythm Track:** #2 **Technique:** Ornaments **Genre:** Any pop style

Description: Today we'll place a quick fall at the end of a note. This gesture is a great way to add a little character to a note and can be very subtle.

Tip: Quickly slide down from the written pitch at the very end of the note. Make the slide an almost unnoticeable part of the note. Try this ornament with different fingers and pitches. Once you have the hang of this, experiment with more dramatic downward slides.

WED

Workout #115 **Rhythm Track:** #5 **Technique:** Rhythm/Feel **Genre:** Any

Description: This exercise focuses on a series of up-bow syncopations. At a fast tempo, it's difficult to keep the notes in time and not allow them to drift onto the beat.

Tip: If you're able, try to listen only to the click of the metronome and keep your playing on autopilot. Listening too much to your own part in a passage like this can get you into trouble as you lose touch with the other players.

THU

Workout #116 **Rhythm Track:** #2 **Technique:** Arpeggios **Genre:** Any

Description: Today we'll play an F7 arpeggio throughout first position.

Tip: You've got a couple of chances to work on your fourth-finger extension today: the C on the E string and the E♭ near the beginning of the third bar. Fingerings like this may seem like quite a reach at first, but being comfortable with them can make many licks and passages much easier.

FRI

Workout #117 **Rhythm Track:** #5 **Technique:** Playing with Others **Genre:** Country

Description: By outlining chords with double stops, a simple melody can reinforce the harmonies and fill out an accompaniment. We'll add a few grace notes, too, to inject some interest.

Tip: Use enough speed in the bow that your sound doesn't get crunchy or choked. Play close attention to your metronome as you practice this. Focusing outside yourself is terrific preparation for accompanying someone else. Playing a simple accompaniment like this leaves room for other instruments.

SAT

Workout #118 **Rhythm Track:** #5 **Technique:** Bowing **Genre:** Rock/Pop

Description: This week we'll practice a short, percussive stroke. We're going for a sound like a drummer playing a fill on the snare drum.

Tip: This bowing is easiest around the middle of the bow. The bow will bounce high off the string and land percussively. It's a rather vertical bow stroke.

SUN

Workout #119 **Rhythm Track:** #2 **Technique:** Stretching Out **Genre:** Latin

About the Example: This short tune should have a relaxed tango feel.

MON

Workout #120   **Rhythm Track:** #6   **Technique:** Scales   **Genre:** Any

Description: Today we'll play a G whole tone scale. A whole tone scale is just what its name implies, a scale made up of whole steps. Do the math and you'll find that there are only six pitches in this scale. It's an exotic sound that takes some extra thought to play on the violin.

Tip: Try the printed fingerings so that you're comfortable with a couple of approaches. Notice that there are only two patterns for the fingerings on a string, one with an open string and one with a low first finger.

TUE

Workout #121   **Rhythm Track:** #2   **Technique:** Ornaments   **Genre:** Any pop style

Description: For the most part, a straight tone is the basic sound in pop music, and vibrato is used as an ornament. Depending on the style, vibrato can be quite common, but it isn't the default tone the way it tends to be in post-Baroque classical music. In this exercise, we'll alternate between a straight tone and a pop-friendly vibrato.

Tip: The first note of each bar uses no vibrato. The dotted-half note adds it. For this exercise, mimic the vibrato a gospel singer might use. The vibrato will be a little slower and wider than would be typical in classical music. Beginning a note with a straight tone and blossoming into vibrato is a useful expressive device, so give that a try as well.

WED

Workout #122   **Rhythm Track:** #4   **Technique:** Rhythm/Feel   **Genre:** Swing/Jazz

Description: When you're swinging, the off-beat eighth notes in bars 1 and 3 happen just before the next beat. Notes like these are sometimes called "anticipations." This exercise will give you a chance to practice that rhythm. It also introduces a couple of quicker flourishes.

Tip: The grace notes that begin the exercise and the 32nd notes in bar 2 go by quickly. Think of them as ornaments to the note that follows. Check out the recording for guidance.

Workout #123 **Rhythm Track:** #6 **Technique:** Arpeggios **Genre:** Any

Description: B major can be a tricky key to play in. You might find that many licks are easier to play if you use the "box" concept introduced in Week 16. Here's a chance to play a major arpeggio using a pattern that you can move all over the fingerboard.

Tip: Part of the point of the left-hand "box" idea is that we're not reliant on open strings. Because of this, you can move your hand up or down the fingerboard like a guitarist without having to rethink licks you've been practicing. Try moving your hand back to B♭ or up to D♭ and using this same left-hand pattern.

FRI

Workout #124 **Rhythm Track:** #2 **Technique:** Playing with Others **Genre:** Pop

Description: Let's use some double stops and constant eighth notes to create a driving pop rhythm.

Tip: Play this in the lower part of the bow, near the frog. Use a slower, weightier bow to catch the string and help the notes to sound meaty.

SAT

Workout #125 **Rhythm Track:** #2 **Technique:** Bowing **Genre:** Funk/Rock

Description: In this exercise, we're going for a pronounced, quick attack on every note. Imagine the sound of a funk horn section. Or, better yet, check out some recordings of Earth, Wind & Fire. That's the sound we're aiming for.

Tip: Play in the middle to lower part of the bow and let the bow bounce way off the string. It's fine to get some extra grit in the sound. You want these notes to really pop out.

SUN

Workout #126 **Rhythm Track:** #2 **Technique:** Stretching Out **Genre:** Pop

About the Example: Here's a big casserole of a lot of the techniques we've been working on. Eat up!

MON

Workout #127   **Rhythm Track:** #2   **Technique:** Scales   **Genre:** Any
Description: Let's work on playing octaves with a G melodic minor scale.
Tip: Aside from the notes that use an open string, we'll use the same first and fourth finger grip for every double stop. To begin, play only the lower note of each pair, with the printed fingering. We'll be doing a lot of shifting, so keep your left hand relaxed. Octaves tend to sound fuller and to be easier to tune if you put more emphasis on the lower pitch.

TUE

Workout #128   **Rhythm Track:** #4   **Technique:** Ornaments   **Genre:** Any pop style
Description: Let's try an ornament often called a "shake." This is a gesture you might hear from the lead trumpet in a loud big band passage. Check out the recording to better understand what you're going for.
Tip: Instead of rolling your finger like a normal vibrato, slide your finger along the string. Put an accent on each note and taper the end of the bow stroke. Increase the width of the shake as you release the weight of the bow at the end of the note.

WED

Workout #129   **Rhythm Track:** #2   **Technique:** Rhythm/Feel   **Genre:** Funk/Pop
Description: This is a good exercise for keeping your rhythm steady as you alternate between short, syncopated offbeats and longer slurs. Keep the offbeats strictly in time, even though you're switching between up- and down-bows.
Tip: Feel the contrast between the offbeat notes and the grounded, on-the-beat figure in the second half of the first bar. Keep the syncopated notes short.

THU

Workout #130   **Rhythm Track:** #5   **Technique:** Arpeggios   **Genre:** Any

Description: Today's exercise is pretty straightforward and will allow more practice on the minor 7th chord, this time with C as the root.

Tip: Today we're starting at the bottom of the violin's range instead of the root. This will give you a chance to explore all the notes in first position for this chord.

FRI

Workout #131   **Rhythm Track:** #4   **Technique:** Playing with Others   **Genre:** Jazz/Swing

Description: Here's a jazzy vamp to work on your comping skills. "Comping" is short for "accompanying." The term is most often used in jazz. It's often a chordal figure that supports a melody or soloist.

Tip: Play the quarter notes with separation and stay rhythmic. The chords are important, but the rhythm and feel, even on something as basic as repeated quarter notes, is what matters most in this music. The "reversed" bowing helps to bring out the accents on beats 2 and 4.

SAT

Workout #132   **Rhythm Track:** #2   **Technique:** Bowing   **Genre:** Any

Description: Today we'll focus on string crossings played both slurred and separate.

Tip: Keep your rhythm perfectly even throughout. Practice the first beat by itself. Keep the weight in your bow arm and sustain your sound on the slurs. When this feels comfortable, add the rest of the exercise.

SUN

Workout #133   **Rhythm Track:** #4   **Technique:** Stretching Out   **Genre:** Swing

About the Example: Today we'll play a short tune in D♭. If you're having trouble with intonation, review the D♭ major scale slowly, using your tuner.

MON

Workout #134   **Rhythm Track:** #2   **Technique:** Scales   **Genre:** Any

Description: Playing scales in thirds is a terrific technique builder. Today we'll use C melodic minor.

Tip: Think ahead about what interval the next double stop is. You may want to begin practicing this exercise by playing the bottom pitch and then adding the upper note for each double stop. Use a drone on C to help keep your pitch grounded.

TUE

Workout #135   **Rhythm Track:** #5   **Technique:** Ornaments   **Genre:** Any pop style

Description: Let's combine our two chop strokes into an eighth-note rhythm.

Tip: Dampen the strings with your left hand so that you get an unpitched, percussive sound. On the accented notes, try chopping on the higher strings, a bit toward the fingerboard, to get more variety of sound and to bring out beats 2 and 4.

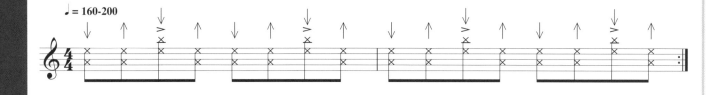

WED

Workout #136   **Rhythm Track:** #4   **Technique:** Rhythm/Feel   **Genre:** Blues/Swing

Description: This exercise forces you to be as swinging as you can as you switch between anticipations and on-the-beat figures. You also get a chance to work on your shake.

Tip: Pay close attention to when you arrive on beat 2. There'll be just a bit of separation after the anticipation with the shake. Make sure it feels right and don't rush. If you'd like to, try experimenting with playing everything just a little late to the beat. This concept is part of what can make a figure sound loose and relaxed.

THU

Workout #137   **Rhythm Track:** #2   **Technique:** Arpeggios   **Genre:** Any

Description: Today we'll play a number of double stops up into third position on an E7 chord.

Tip: The seconds and sevenths presented here can add a lot of interest to a passage. They're a lot less commonly heard on the violin than thirds or sixths and can really spice things up.

FRI

Workout #138   **Rhythm Track:** #1   **Technique:** Playing with Others   **Genre:** Pop

Description: Here's another exercise using double stops to outline a chord progression.

Tip: Make a distinct beginning and end on each note. Stay in the string and hold each note for its full value without dissipating the sound. Try to make the end of each note as rhythmic as the beginning.

SAT

Workout #139   **Rhythm Track:** #5   **Technique:** Bowing   **Genre:** Any

Description: Today's exercise is a six-notes-to-a-beat figure called a sextuplet. At a quick tempo it's flashy and fun to play, so today we'll work on speed.

Tip: Start at a comfortable pace and slowly increase the tempo as much as you're able. You want to get to the point where the sextuplet feels like a single gesture or group rather than a slew of individual notes. For a trickier exercise, start up-bow.

SUN

Workout #140   **Rhythm Track:** #5   **Technique:** Stretching Out   **Genre:** Blues

About the Example: Here's a chance to practice our "box position" idea. Play everything in fourth position.

MON

Workout #141   **Rhythm Track:** #2   **Technique:** Scales   **Genre:** Any

Description: This exercise is similar to those in Weeks 8 and 13, but today we'll play tenths. (A tenth is the interval of an octave plus a third.) This exercise will help your intonation and is a great help to developing a good hand frame and the use of your left elbow.

Tip: Keep each finger down as long as possible. The idea is to have your left hand act as though it were playing double-stops that are two or three strings apart. Play very slowly and try to make your intonation perfect. Keep a drone sounding in the background on G to keep yourself honest. Check the tuning of your open G before you start.

TUE

Workout #142   **Rhythm Track:** #5   **Technique:** Ornaments   **Genre:** Any pop style

Description: Let's use our chops from last week and add a little swing to the rhythm.

Tip: Dampen the strings with the fingers of your left hand. Their placement isn't important. You'll have to change the angle of your bow quickly to get from an up-chop on the lower strings to the down-chop on the higher strings for the accents. Try playing the accented, upper-string notes a little farther away from the bridge than the rest of the figure.

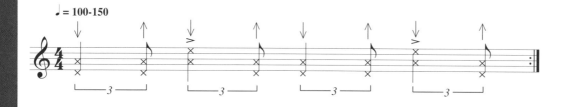

WED

Workout #143   **Rhythm Track:** #5   **Technique:** Rhythm/Feel   **Genre:** Any

Description: This exercise is tricky to play quickly because your ear can start hearing this short offbeat scale as falling on the beat. The bowing might take some concentration to internalize as well.

Tip: As much as possible, listen exclusively to the click so that you're reacting to it instead of listening to your own playing. This is difficult to do at first, but this skill will allow you to play with others and immediately adjust to any fluctuations in the tempo.

Workout #144 **Rhythm Track:** #5 **Technique:** Arpeggios **Genre:** Any

Description: This exercise spells out a G diminished 7th chord. This chord is sometimes called "fully diminished" to distinguish it from a half-diminished chord, but that isn't necessary. It is described as "symmetrical" because every interval is a minor third (three half steps). Because of this, there are functionally only three diminished 7th chords. The other nine are simply inversions, the same pitches beginning on a different note, of those three chords.

Tip: Tritones are always a little tricky on the violin. Players interested in orchestral music easily understand why the scherzo movement from Robert Schumann's Symphony No. 2 is an infamous audition excerpt. Go slowly at first and concentrate on playing this exercise perfectly in tune.

Workout #145 **Rhythm Track:** #4 **Technique:** Playing with Others **Genre:** Jazz/Swing

Description: Let's play a jazz accompaniment using pizzicato.

Tip: Hold the violin in guitar position and use your thumb to play this. Put a little separation between the notes by partially releasing the pressure of the fingers of your left hand. Keep the rhythm steady and bring out the accents. Even though it's just quarter notes, make it swing.

Workout #146 **Rhythm Track:** #7 **Technique:** Bowing **Genre:** Bluegrass/Cajun

Description: This is another common bowing in fiddle playing. The left hand is going about its business playing constant eighth notes, but the right hand does a repeating slurring pattern that adds a cool rhythmic spice to the passage.

Tip: On the single, accented bow, you'll need to use a fast, light stroke so that you can recover the same amount of bow that you use on the three slurred notes; otherwise, you'll find yourself running out of bow. You can also try playing this with a bit of swinging lilt.

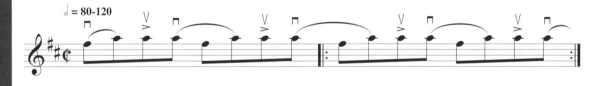

Workout #147 **Rhythm Track:** #4 **Technique:** Stretching Out **Genre:** Blues/Swing

About the Example: This riff puts together a number of the techniques we've practiced, but the most important thing to do when you play it is make it swing and feel good.

MON

Workout #148   **Rhythm Track:** #2   **Technique:** Scales   **Genre:** Any

Description: This exercise will help to solidify the Dorian scale in your ears and fingers. We're playing the notes of C Dorian and putting them into a pattern of fourths.

Tip: As you play this exercise, think about the intervallic relationship of the notes. Pay attention to the spot in the scale where the fourth is augmented (E♭ up to A♮ in this example). This will streamline your thought process when you want to play this pattern in other keys.

TUE

Workout #149   **Rhythm Track:** #4   **Technique:** Ornaments   **Genre:** Any pop style

Description: Today we'll play a quick slide down from our main note.

Tip: Begin the slide on the "and" of beat 1. This gesture should be very quick. Listening to the recording will help you to understand the sound you're going for.

WED

Workout #150   **Rhythm Track:** #4   **Technique:** Rhythm/Feel   **Genre:** Swing/Jazz

Description: This is a terrific exercise to work on your feel as you make a big string crossing and alternate between single and double stops.

Tip: Make sure you finish your string crossing before you start your up-bow as you alternate registers. This will keep your playing sounding clean.

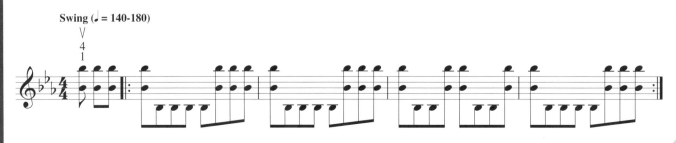

THU

Workout #151   **Rhythm Track:** #2   **Technique:** Arpeggios   **Genre:** Any

Description: Let's work on some double stops for a B♭7 chord. Jazz tunes are often in flat keys like E♭, A♭, and F, so this exercise will serve you well. There are some tricky rearrangements of the fingers in the left hand. Go slowly until you're comfortable.

Tip: Much of this exercise is in what is considered "half position." (Your first finger is halfway between first position and the nut.) Playing there can feel a little awkward at first, but in time will feel familiar. You may want to begin by playing the bottom note of each pair alone and then adding in the upper pitch. Play with a drone on B♭ if you can – to keep yourself honest.

FRI

Workout #152   **Rhythm Track:** #2   **Technique:** Playing with Others   **Genre:** Rock

Description: Today we're going for a heavy, aggressive sound.

Tip: Play close to the frog and let the bow bounce far off the string. Grab the string and immediately lift to create a space between the notes.

SAT

Workout #153   **Rhythm Track:** #7   **Technique:** Bowing   **Genre:** Bluegrass/Cajun

Description: This example is a lot like last week's, but now we're going to reverse the bowing. This might feel awkward at first, but it makes playing the accents on the "ands" of the beat much easier and more natural.

Tip: If your down-bows are too loud because you're trying to recover the longer bow you use on the preceding three eighths, use a light stroke so that the accents aren't too overwhelming. Add a tiny bit of swing to make this feel looser.

SUN

Workout #154   **Rhythm Track:** #4   **Technique:** Stretching Out   **Genre:** Blues/Swing

About the Example: There are a number of techniques to incorporate into this riff. Go slowly until everything feels comfortable.

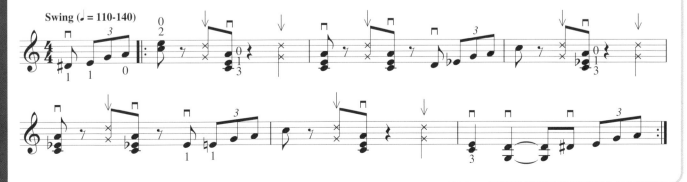

MON

Workout #155 **Rhythm Track:** #5 **Technique:** Scales **Genre:** Any
Description: Let's revisit the Mixolydian scale, this time in D. We'll play in first and third position for this etude.
Tip: If you're not yet comfortable with shifting, find an exercise to get used to it. In the meantime, play as high as you're comfortable. Try practicing a number of fingerings so that you have options when a passage like this comes up.

TUE

Workout #156 **Rhythm Track:** #5 **Technique:** Ornaments **Genre:** Any pop style
Description: Let's put a couple of ornaments together. We'll slide up to the first note and add a shake. On the following two notes we'll play a bend up and a fall down.
Tip: Start the notes with the slide on the beat and well below the D we're arriving on. Take your time getting there for a nice greasy slide!

WED

Workout #157 **Rhythm Track:** #4 **Technique:** Rhythm/Feel **Genre:** Swing/Blues
Description: Here's a hip two-bar pattern to work on your swing feel.
Tip: As you play, make sure you keep a relaxed, lazy feel. Play a little late to the beat, with your notes sounding just a tiny bit after the click of the metronome. That way of playing can give swing music part of its laid-back, cool sound.

THU

Workout #158 **Rhythm Track:** #3 **Technique:** Arpeggios **Genre:** Any

Description: An augmented (or #5) chord is a major triad with its fifth raised by a half step. In the case of an A augmented chord, the fifth is raised from E to E♯.

Tip: Playing an E♯ on the violin can feel weird at first. The exercise is written using that pitch because it's the standard way to notate this chord. It may be easier, though, to think of playing an F. The two notes are enharmonic, meaning they're two spellings of the same pitch. Over time, this will become comfortable.

FRI

Workout #159 **Rhythm Track:** #4 **Technique:** Playing with Others **Genre:** Swing

Description: Let's add some ghost notes to a standard swing figure to create a four-bar riff. The ghosted notes can be a pitch or just a rhythmic sound. They should be much quieter than the regular notes.

Tip: Repeat the first two bars until they feel comfortable. Then, at a slow tempo, loop just the fourth bar until the bowing and ghost notes sound good. Then you can put everything together.

SAT

Workout #160 **Rhythm Track:** #2 **Technique:** Bowing **Genre:** Funk/Pop

Description: This week we're mimicking a funk guitar riff. We want a good, biting attack to each note.

Tip: The notes can ring for a moment and should then be dampened by releasing the pressure of the fingers of the left hand, but keeping them in contact with the string.

SUN

Workout #161 **Rhythm Track:** #4 **Technique:** Stretching Out **Genre:** Swing/Jazz

About the Example: We'll use a figure from last week as an intro to a short swing tune in E♭.

MON

Workout #162   **Rhythm Track:** #2   **Technique:** Scales   **Genre:** Any

Description: Now that you've got some experience with the Mixolydian scale, let's aim for more facility and familiarity by playing the scale as a pattern of broken, not double-stopped, sixths.

Tip: This exercise is tricky in that tritones (the F♯ to C) and fifths are both finicky intervals on the violin. Try several fingerings for the tritones to get comfortable with different options. To move across the strings in fifths, it helps to think ahead and place your finger on both pitches by aiming at the fingerboard in between the two strings.

TUE

Workout #163   **Rhythm Track:** #2   **Technique:** Ornaments   **Genre:** Any pop style

Description: Let's put all our chopping concepts together for some funky goodness!

Tip: Start slowly and isolate any part of the exercise that feels tricky. Then put everything together and slowly increase the tempo. Try adding your open A to the pitched double stops for a fuller sound.

WED

Workout #164   **Rhythm Track:** #4   **Technique:** Rhythm/Feel   **Genre:** Blues/Swing

Description: Now that you're getting more experienced with swinging, try this cool little riff.

Tip: Use the printed fingering so that you use your open E along with your fourth finger in third position on the A string. Shout out this figure like a horn section.

THU

Workout #165   **Rhythm Track:** #2   **Technique:** Arpeggios   **Genre:** Any

Description: Here's a series of double stops from a G7 chord. When people say E7 or B♭7, for example, they're talking about a dominant 7th chord. It is like the major 7th chord we looked at in Weeks 6 and 16, but with a ♭7th. That means that the seventh degree is lowered by a half step from where it would be in a major scale.

Tip: This chord goes hand-in-hand with the Mixolydian scale. If you play the odd-numbered notes of a Mixolydian scale (1, 3, 5, 7) you get a dominant 7th chord.

FRI

Workout #166   **Rhythm Track:** #4   **Technique:** Playing with Others   **Genre:** Swing

Description: Here's a standard ending you've probably heard many times.

Tip: This is a handy lick for ending a tune. Check out the movement of the two lines as the top note goes up and the lower note descends.

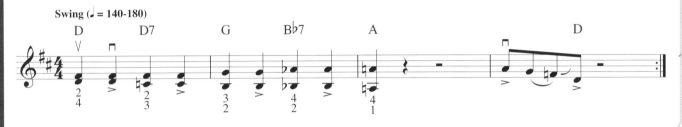

SAT

Workout #167   **Rhythm Track:** #5   **Technique:** Bowing   **Genre:** Any

Description: Let's look at another string-crossing pattern.

Tip: Start practicing this at a tempo that you can play cleanly. As you increase the tempo, use less bow and gradually change from a forearm stroke to one that comes more from your wrist.

SUN

Workout #168   **Rhythm Track:** #7   **Technique:** Stretching Out   **Genre:** Cajun/Bluegrass

About the Example: This riff looks tricky, but all the double stops use an open string.

MON

Workout #169   **Rhythm Track:** #5   **Technique:** Scales   **Genre:** Any

Description: The Mixolydian scale is important in popular music, so it's a great advantage to be comfortable with it. Today we'll practice a little sequence in B♭. This scale goes hand in hand with dominant chords. Today's exercise is the basic scale of a B♭7 chord.

Tip: Once you're comfortable with this, play the notes of the Mixolydian scale in a different order, creating a pattern of your own.

TUE

Workout #170   **Rhythm Track:** #4   **Technique:** Ornaments   **Genre:** Any pop style

Description: Today we'll play some short downward bends.

Tip: Start the note on the beat and immediately bend it down to the written pitch. You can begin the note close to where you want to end up. It's a short distance, only about a quarter step.

WED

Workout #171   **Rhythm Track:** #2   **Technique:** Rhythm/Feel   **Genre:** Country

Description: This exercise is the sort of lick you might hear in a country-rock song.

Tip: Put emphasis on beats 2 and 4, right where that big snare drum goes. If you'd like to play this with more of a bluegrass feel, move the accents to the "and" of each quarter-note beat.

THU

Workout #172   **Rhythm Track:** #2   **Technique:** Arpeggios   **Genre:** Any

Description: Let's start playing some double stops from major 7th chords. Use a B♭ drone to help you stay in tune.

Tip: To begin, play the lower note of each pair by itself, then add the upper note. Once you can do that comfortably, play the exercise slowly as written. There are a couple of unusual intervals here, but you'll be able to do a lot with this sort of thing in the future. Be patient!

FRI

Workout #173   **Rhythm Track:** #2   **Technique:** Playing with Others   **Genre:** Pop

Description: Playing in octaves can add heft to a simple line.

Tip: We'll play each octave pair with our first and fourth fingers. Play just the lower octave notes with the printed fingering first. When you add the upper octave, it will be easier to tune if it's a little quieter and blends into the lower octave.

SAT

Workout #174   **Rhythm Track:** #5   **Technique:** Bowing   **Genre:** Any

Description: Let's do some more work on string crossings to increase fluidity with the bow.

Tip: As always, start slowly, listen to the metronome, and slowly increase speed. Always stay economical. You want to keep your motions as efficient as possible. Once you're playing quickly enough to be moving primarily from your wrist, experiment to see if you can find an upper arm position that makes this motion easier.

SUN

Workout #175   **Rhythm Track:** #4   **Technique:** Stretching Out   **Genre:** Blues/Swing

About the Example: Play this in second position. The slurred triplet should begin on C, bend down a bit to an indistinct pitch, then bend back up to C. Check out the recording to hear what this sounds like.

MON

Workout #176   **Rhythm Track:** #5   **Technique:** Scales   **Genre:** Any

Description: The melodic minor scale is quite useful, and can create a sophisticated jazz sound. It is like the natural minor scale we studied in Week 2, but with raised sixth and seventh degrees. It is also identical to a major scale that's had its third note lowered by a half step.

Tip: We'll be exploring other scales that are derived from this pattern. Try to internalize this scale and play it in sequences and patterns of your own. If you can get comfortable with this scale, you are well on your way to being comfortable in jazz.

TUE

Workout #177   **Rhythm Track:** #5   **Technique:** Ornaments   **Genre:** Any pop style

Description: Today we'll slide both pitches of a double stop. A gesture like this is common in country music.

Tip: Since both pitches are moving, you can slide your whole hand up, like a short shift. The slide itself will begin close to the main pitch and on the beat. Because this is a country lick, try a slower, relaxed vibrato.

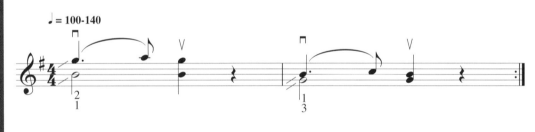

WED

Workout #178   **Rhythm Track:** #4   **Technique:** Rhythm/Feel   **Genre:** Swing/Blues

Description: This exercise introduces a pair of 16th notes where you'd normally have one eighth note. Make sure your swing feel stays swinging.

Tip: You may be tempted to begin the 16ths a little early. Stick to your guns and create a great swing feel!

THU

Workout #179   **Rhythm Track:** #5   **Technique:** Arpeggios   **Genre:** Any

Description: Here's an interesting pattern. We're using the notes of a diminished chord as the roots of ascending dominant chords. This device, a sequence moving by contiguous minor thirds, is fairly common in music with jazz influences. It can add harmonic spice to a tune or solo.

Tip: Once you've gotten the hang of this exercise, play a different four-note pattern up by contiguous minor thirds. It's an excellent brainteaser and you may discover some cool sounds.

FRI

Workout #180   **Rhythm Track:** #5   **Technique:** Playing with Others   **Genre:** Pop

Description: Today we'll play a version of a standard swing and early rock lick. Listen to the recording to better understand what you're going for.

Tip: The open G and D string notes are there to fill out the riff and add some rhythmic interest. They're less important than the moving notes. Swallow the open string double stops a little. They're part of the underlying rhythm but less important, and should be softer, than the moving line.

SAT

Workout #181   **Rhythm Track:** #4   **Technique:** Bowing   **Genre:** Swing

Description: In this exercise we're practicing our "stopped bow" technique from Week 2, but applying it to a swing feel.

Tip: The written triplet rhythm doesn't need to be exact, just go for a good swing feel. The marked end to each note is important, though. Make the stopping of the bow an integral part of this rhythm. This is a subtle thing to hear, but the feeling is important. It's these little touches that make the music feel right.

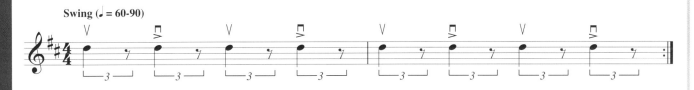

SUN

Workout #182   **Rhythm Track:** #5   **Technique:** Stretching Out   **Genre:** Blues

About the Example: This figure uses our box approach in second position. Once you've got this lick, try moving it to a different key.

55

WEEK 27

MON

Workout #183   **Rhythm Track:** #2   **Technique:** Scales   **Genre:** Any

Description: Today we'll play the E Dorian scale. This exercise will take us up into fourth position. There are a couple of fingerings in the example. Try them both so that you're comfortable getting around the fingerboard in different ways.

Tip: If you'd like to, play the whole exercise in fourth position. Playing across all four strings in an upper position is excellent practice.

TUE

Workout #184   **Rhythm Track:** #2   **Technique:** Ornaments   **Genre:** Any pop style

Description: Let's combine a bend down with one that moves up. The main pitch is the ♭5 in C. Start and end the note just above that, close to a G♮.

Tip: Start the note right on the beat, a little higher than the G♭. Hold the main note for its full value, then bend it back up right on the next eighth-note subdivision, the eighth rest. The recording will make this easier to understand.

WED

Workout #185   **Rhythm Track:** #2   **Technique:** Rhythm/Feel   **Genre:** Rock/Funk

Description: Today we'll practice being precise with a somewhat unwieldy bow stroke.

Tip: To make this passage sound good, you need a vertical, percussive bow stroke. At the same time, it needs to be precisely in rhythm – even when crossing strings. Extra grit in the sound is just fine. Dampen the open strings with your left hand if they're ringing too much.

THU

Workout #186   **Rhythm Track:** #5   **Technique:** Arpeggios   **Genre:** Any

Description: E7 has long been the chord of choice for extended solo sections in bands with guitar. You will play over this chord a lot, so let's get comfortable.

Tip: Tritones are the most important part of a dominant chord's sound, but they're a little tricky to play in tune at first. In this example, pay attention to the G♯ and D on the middle two strings and try the printed fingering. At first, this might feel less comfortable than using your third finger for both notes, but this fingering will eventually allow you to play more quickly and smoothly.

FRI

Workout #187   **Rhythm Track:** #2   **Technique:** Playing with Others   **Genre:** Rock/Pop

Description: Here we're outlining some chords like those you might find in a pop or rock song.

Tip: Play this off the string near the frog. Aim for the middle string with your bow. Be aggressive and precise.

SAT

Workout #188   **Rhythm Track:** #2   **Technique:** Bowing   **Genre:** Any pop style

Description: Okay, today we're going to get a little fancier with our bowing exercise. We'll combine a number of the concepts we've been practicing.

Tip: Go for a clipped funk sound. At the end of each note you'll need to release the weight of the bow as you bring it to a halt. Otherwise, your sound can get too crunchy.

SUN

Workout #189   **Rhythm Track:** #2   **Technique:** Stretching Out   **Genre:** Rock

About the Example: Play the dotted notes aggressively and off the string. We're going for a big, blues-rock sound.

WEEK 28

MON

Workout #190   **Rhythm Track:** #2   **Technique:** Scales   **Genre:** Any

Description: Here's a great exercise to get the G melodic minor scale in your ear and fingers. Playing a scale in broken sixths like this is an effective way to become more comfortable with the sound and patterns of a scale. The melodic minor is a valuable scale. As you become conversant with it, you'll be better equipped to create some of the sophisticated sounds that jazz can deliver.

Tip: Pay attention to the pattern of the intervals as you practice this. Try playing this sequence in a different key; the relationships will all be the same. If you have trouble, write out the scale in the new key. This will help you understand what you need to.

TUE

Workout #191   **Rhythm Track:** #2   **Technique:** Ornaments   **Genre:** Any pop style

Description: This exercise begins by bending a note up and then back down. It has a cool, bluesy sound.

Tip: First, practice each part of the lick separately. Repeat the first part of the lick (up to the D on the second beat) slowly, without the bend. Once you've got that, add the bend. When that feels good, put the whole lick together.

WED

Workout #192   **Rhythm Track:** #4   **Technique:** Rhythm/Feel   **Genre:** Swing

Description: This exercise is designed to help develop your swing feel with the added element of string crossings and a bowing that reverses because of its three-against-two rhythm.

Tip: Start practicing this slowly, paying close attention to the click of the metronome. You can use either the open A string or your fourth finger on the D string to get a slightly different bowing pattern. Try it both ways. The more ways you can practice this, the better.

THU

Workout #193   **Rhythm Track:** #2   **Technique:** Arpeggios   **Genre:** Any

Description: Minor 7th chords also spell a sonority called the "major 6 chord." Today's E♭m7 exercise does double duty as a G♭6 arpeggio. It's a good thing; this isn't the easiest key on the violin.

Tip: The two fifths in the last bar can be difficult to play in tune, especially the first one. Let your third finger move together with your pinkie to give it more strength. Use the fleshy part of your pinkie, but don't let the joints of your finger collapse.

FRI

Workout #194   **Rhythm Track:** #2   **Technique:** Playing with Others   **Genre:** Pop

Description: This exercise pairs some offbeat chops with a common pop cliché.

Tip: Play the double stops alone, first at a slow tempo, then add in the chops. Once you feel comfortable, you can increase the tempo.

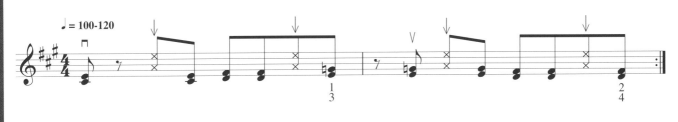

SAT

Workout #195   **Rhythm Track:** #5   **Technique:** Bowing   **Genre:** Any

Description: Here's another string-crossing exercise to work on your bowing efficiency.

Tip: This one can make you dizzy! Go slowly until you understand the mechanics involved, then gradually speed things up.

SUN

Workout #196   **Rhythm Track:** #2   **Technique:** Stretching Out   **Genre:** Blues/Roots

About the Example: Give a listen to the recording if this example looks confusing. You can play straight time or give the 16th notes a little swing, as on the recording.

MON

Workout #197 **Rhythm Track:** #2 **Technique:** Scales **Genre:** Any

Description: A diminished chord is built using only minor thirds (three half-steps). This scale is derived from that chord. In effect, this scale is simply two diminished 7th chords stacked next to each other. (If you dissect this exercise, you'll find a G diminished chord and an A diminished chord.) Because of the diminished scale's symmetrical nature, there are only three versions before the pattern repeats.

Tip: This is a useful scale, but it can feel awkward at first on the violin. It might also be tricky to play by ear, so go slowly and be aware of the repeating pattern of a whole step followed by a half step. This is the scale that works most easily over diminished 7th chords.

TUE

Workout #198 **Rhythm Track:** #2 **Technique:** Ornaments **Genre:** Any pop style

Description: Here's an idiomatic ornament that works in most any style: a double stop made of an open string combined with a slide up to the unison pitch on a lower string.

Tip: The slide doesn't have to be very far, but you'll need to end right on the pitch of the open string and hold it. If you're accidentally hitting the open string with your finger, make sure your fingers are curved over the open string. Bringing your left elbow under the violin and making sure your wrist isn't collapsed will help.

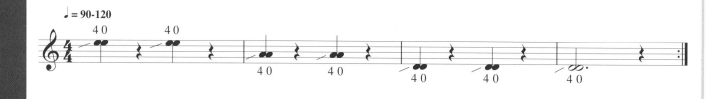

WED

Workout #199 **Rhythm Track:** #4 **Technique:** Rhythm/Feel **Genre:** Swing

Description: This exercise uses a common rhythm called the Charleston. The rhythm was popularized in mainstream dance music in the U.S. by a 1923 tune, "The Charleston," by pianist/composer Jimmie Johnson; the lyrics were written by Cecil Mack.

Tip: Make sure the second note of each bar is short and quick. Keep repeating this rhythm with your metronome or backing track and see how danceable you can make it.

THU

Workout #200   **Rhythm Track:** #2   **Technique:** Arpeggios   **Genre:** Any

Description: A minor 7th chord is built with the odd-numbered notes of a minor scale. In the case of this A minor 7th chord, the pitches are A, C, E, and G. You might see this chord written Amin7 or Am7.

Tip: Because the upper notes of a minor 7th chord form a major triad, you may recognize some double stops in this exercise that sound like part of a C major chord. If this exercise feels tricky, play each pair one note at a time as eighth notes.

FRI

Workout #201   **Rhythm Track:** #7   **Technique:** Playing with Others   **Genre:** Bluegrass

Description: To signal the end of a tune, you can play a standard "tag" that is the universal fiddle announcement of "We're done!" This is what's written for the first two bars.

Tip: If ending a tune with just those two bars sounds too abrupt, you can fill things out for another two bars with something like the second half of this exercise.

SAT

Workout #202   **Rhythm Track:** #5   **Technique:** Bowing   **Genre:** Any

Description: This is a neat little rhythmic figure that's also a great bowing exercise.

Tip: Start at the tip and work your way down to the frog during the first measure. Then, with the same articulation, work your way back to the tip in bar 2.

SUN

Workout #203   **Rhythm Track:** #7   **Technique:** Stretching Out   **Genre:** Bluegrass

About the Example: Here's a cool, up-tempo bluegrass melody with a little surprise from a 3/4 bar. Sometimes a melody with a rhythmic hitch like this is referred to as "crooked."

MON

Workout #204 **Rhythm Track:** #5 **Technique:** Scales **Genre:** Any

Description: There are two ways to arrange a diminished scale: a repeating pattern of a whole step followed by a half step – a "whole-half" diminished scale – and the reverse – the "half-whole" diminished scale. Today's scale is derived from an A whole-half diminished scale.

Tip: The pitches of this scale spell whole-half diminished scales beginning on A, C, Eb, and Gb, and half-whole scales that begin on B, D, F, and Ab. This might seem confusing at first, but it means that you've done a lot today!

TUE

Workout #205 **Rhythm Track:** #2 **Technique:** Ornaments **Genre:** Any pop style

Description: We can give a little oomph to notes on the upper three strings with what might be called a "scrape" or "rake."

Tip: The grace notes can be either pitched notes that are immediately choked by releasing the pressure in your left hand, or unpitched notes played by dampening the strings so that the pitch isn't apparent.

WED

Workout #206 **Rhythm Track:** #2 **Technique:** Rhythm/Feel **Genre:** Any pop style

Description: Here's an interesting pattern. It's a seven-note figure that gets repeated so that, within four bars, it begins on each of the four 16th-note subdivisions.

Tip: Play this in the lower half of the bow – near the frog – with a short, off-the-string articulation. Keep listening to the click of your metronome!

THU

Workout #207   **Rhythm Track:** #3   **Technique:** Arpeggios   **Genre:** Any

Description: To get really comfortable with our "box" position idea, try these double stops in second position. Because we're not using open strings, you can move these left-hand shapes to other keys very easily.

Tip: Use a drone on your tuner or app, set to B. It will help keep you grounded as you practice this exercise. Once you're comfortable, move this pattern up the neck and play it in a new key.

FRI

Workout #208   **Rhythm Track:** #4   **Technique:** Playing with Others   **Genre:** Swing

Description: Here's a little shout-chorus-style riff. A shout chorus is a big, exciting climax – usually at the end of a big band arrangement.

Tip: Try to mimic the sound of a big band at full throttle. The quarter notes can be accented and have some separation. This should be loud and joyful!

SAT

Workout #209   **Rhythm Track:** #5   **Technique:** Bowing   **Genre:** Any

Description: More bowing aerobics! This example is trickier than it looks and is good practice.

Tip: As with our previous string-crossing exercises, start slowly then see how quickly you can play while staying efficient and in control.

SUN

Workout #210   **Rhythm Track:** #4   **Technique:** Stretching Out   **Genre:** Swing/Blues

About the Example: As always, listening to the recording is important. It will help you decipher all these different ornaments.

MON

Workout #211 **Rhythm Track:** #2 **Technique:** Scales **Genre:** Any
Description: Playing scales as double stops is terrific practice. Today we'll play the A melodic minor scale in sixths.
Tip: You may want to begin by playing the bottom note of each pair and holding it while adding in the upper pitch. You can also practice each pair one note at a time, first the bottom pitch and then the top, as eighth notes.

TUE

Workout #212 **Rhythm Track:** #4 **Technique:** Ornaments **Genre:** Any pop style
Description: Today we're going to practice a little nudge of the pitch by bending a note up by about a quarter-step and then immediately coming back down to where we started.
Tip: A quarter-step isn't very far! You just want a little nudge.

WED

Workout #213 **Rhythm Track:** #2 **Technique:** Rhythm/Feel **Genre:** Pop
Description: Today's exercise is a triple-stop figure with a quick change to a chop on beat 2.
Tip: Make the dotted rhythm sound snappy. At first it might be difficult to get from the up-bow to the chop. Keep working and it will come! Be sure not to rush the tempo overall. The chops will be a little crisper if you play them on the upper strings.

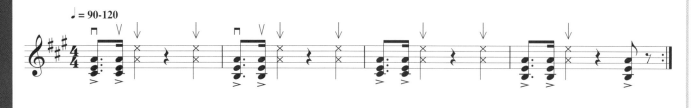

THU

Workout #214   **Rhythm Track:** #5   **Technique:** Arpeggios   **Genre:** Any

Description: Today we'll play a pattern of dominant chords that descend by minor thirds. This exercise uses different chords, but is similar to the ascending pattern we learned in Week 26.

Tip: See if you can create a pattern of your own by playing dominant chords that descend by a different interval.

FRI

Workout #215   **Rhythm Track:** #4   **Technique:** Playing with Others   **Genre:** Blues/Swing

Description: In this riff we're playing some hits in the first bar and a fill in the second bar.

Tip: Get back to the frog quickly for the chop on beat 2. Try to make beat 4 of bar 1 sound as though you're both chopping and playing the pitched notes, like two voices.

SAT

Workout #216   **Rhythm Track:** #2   **Technique:** Bowing   **Genre:** Pop

Description: This is meant to be as close as possible to a quadruple stop. It's not really possible to fully pull this off, but going for it can be a cool sound.

Tip: Bowing on more than two strings is easier if you play toward the fingerboard, where the angle of the strings is flatter. Playing loudly helps a lot, too. You'll want to immediately deaden the strings with your left hand so that they don't ring. We're going for very short notes.

SUN

Workout #217   **Rhythm Track:** #7   **Technique:** Stretching Out   **Genre:** Bluegrass

About the Example: Here's one possibility of how you might kick off a bluegrass tune in B major.

MON

Workout #218 **Rhythm Track:** #5 **Technique:** Scales **Genre:** Any

Description: Today's exercise takes us all over the range of the violin. If you're not yet comfortable in fourth position, you can skip the highest notes of the exercise. You'll still have a great chance to get familiar with the Mixolydian scale in E.

Tip: Shift to fourth position at different points, or play all but the last few notes of the exercise in fourth position. (You'd begin on the G string with your second finger.)

TUE

Workout #219 **Rhythm Track:** #2 **Technique:** Ornaments **Genre:** Any pop style

Description: Today we'll practice bending on a double stop, but we're going to bend only one note. Use your fourth finger to bend the E♭ up approximately a quarter step.

Tip: Slide your pinkie up to bend the E♭, but keep your second finger in place.

WED

Workout #220 **Rhythm Track:** #7 **Technique:** Rhythm/Feel **Genre:** Bluegrass

Description: This is a bowing that can make fiddle tunes more interesting and help bring out the accents on the "ands" of the beat.

Tip: To start, play the example with straight-eighth notes, then add a tiny bit of a swing. Go slowly until you can play this bowing without too much thought, then speed it up.

THU

Workout #221   **Rhythm Track:** #2   **Technique:** Arpeggios   **Genre:** Any

Description: This is an example of double stops that outline a Gmin7♭5 chord.

Tip: This exercise is pretty straightforward. Set up a drone on G and concentrate on your intonation.

FRI

Workout #222   **Rhythm Track:** #4   **Technique:** Playing with Others   **Genre:** Jazz/Swing

Description: To comp in a jazz tune, try playing double stops that outline the chords.

Tip: Put a little accent on beats 2 and 4 in each bar. We're mimicking the sort of approach that guitarists often use in jazz. Check out Freddie Green playing with Count Basie.

SAT

Workout #223   **Rhythm Track:** #2   **Technique:** Bowing   **Genre:** Funk

Description: Here's a little funk figure to try. Go for the bottom strings of the chords and grab the open strings if you can. Keep your rhythm spot-on for the single notes.

Tip: Start each measure with the bow on the string. (Play away from the bridge to get all four strings to sound in the chords.) The single notes should start on the string, with weight in a stopped bow, then pop off the string with a quick stroke that lets the string ring momentarily.

SUN

Workout #224   **Rhythm Track:** #4   **Technique:** Stretching Out   **Genre:** Jazz

About the Example: This exercise will give you an idea of how B diminished arpeggios can work well with a G7♭9 chord.

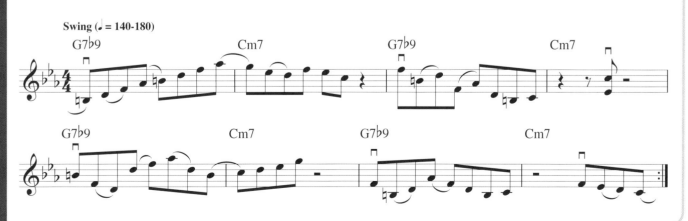

MON

Workout #225   **Rhythm Track:** #5   **Technique:** Scales   **Genre:** Any
Description: Today we'll work on the C Dorian scale. This scale is closely related to the major scale. Dorian is the pattern of intervals created by beginning on the second note of a major scale, or D to D on the white notes of the piano.
Tip: Try using different fingerings to get around the fingerboard, or play all but the last three notes in third position. You can employ scales to work on rhythms or bowings you'd like to improve. Do that today with a feel or articulation you'd like to practice.

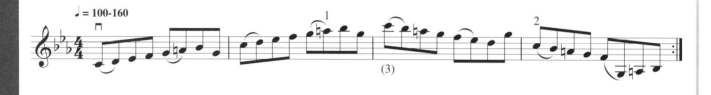

TUE

Workout #226   **Rhythm Track:** #4   **Technique:** Ornaments   **Genre:** Any pop style
Description: Today we'll combine a slide up with a slide down.
Tip: Each quarter note should last for its full value. Begin the note right on the beat and quickly slide up to the written pitch. Hold the note until the rest, then quickly slide down and release the weight of the bow. When you're comfortable, play this ornament with your other fingers.

WED

Workout #227   **Rhythm Track:** #4   **Technique:** Rhythm/Feel   **Genre:** Swing
Description: Here's a chance to work on your swing feel with some string crossings and grace notes.
Tip: Make sure your swing rhythms are solid, even when you're crossing strings in the slurs. Treat the grace notes like an ornament and put the emphasis on the eighth note that follows them.

THU

Workout #228   **Rhythm Track:** #2   **Technique:** Arpeggios   **Genre:** Any

Description: This exercise explores the G♯5 (G augmented) triad. This is an example of a "symmetrical" chord, meaning that all the notes are equidistant. (This is also true of diminished 7th chords.) There are only four ♯5 triads; after that, they begin to repeat with a different root.

Tip: For this chord, all the basic double stops are intervals of either a major third or an augmented fifth. This chord has a powerful sound, but playing it takes a bit of getting used to.

FRI

Workout #229   **Rhythm Track:** #5   **Technique:** Playing with Others   **Genre:** Cajun

Description: Here's an exercise using accented and unaccented notes to create a good feel. It's a bluesy, Cajun-tinged lick.

Tip: Bring out the accents. The other notes can be ghosted or swallowed (i.e., played very quietly). This rhythm is almost straight, but there's a tiny bit of swing in the 16th notes. Go for a kind of lazy, almost-straight shuffle.

SAT

Workout #230   **Rhythm Track:** #2   **Technique:** Bowing   **Genre:** Any pop style

Description: This etude lets you work on keeping a tight, grooving, syncopated rhythm.

Tip: Keep your ear glued to the metronome and place your notes exactly in time. Put a tiny accent at the beginning of each bow for extra definition.

SUN

Workout #231   **Rhythm Track:** #3   **Technique:** Stretching Out   **Genre:** Pop

About the Example: Let's visit the French Riviera and eat some baguettes! Keep everything sustained and lyrical.

MON

Workout #232   **Rhythm Track:** #2   **Technique:** Scales   **Genre:** Any

Description: Today we'll play a pattern derived from a B♭ half-whole diminished scale. Between today's exercise and those from Weeks 29 and 30 (Pages 60 and 62) you'll have tackled the three possible diminished scales. Any other diminished scale you encounter will be a version of one of these three exercises.

Tip: When playing diminished passages, it's helpful to use a fingering that isn't married to each pitch. Instead, be flexible and use the fingering that works well for that part of the passage. On the way up, you're playing major thirds moving by minor thirds; on the way down you're playing perfect fourths moving by minor thirds. Play the scale backward to get more from this exercise.

TUE

Workout #233   **Rhythm Track:** #2   **Technique:** Ornaments   **Genre:** Any pop style

Description: A harmonic is a note played by lightly touching the string. If you play a long bow while very lightly sliding your finger along the G string, you will hear a succession of high-pitched, otherworldly sounds. You can learn how to find these different pitches and add them to your playing.

Tip: The notes with the "O" above them are harmonics. Lightly touch your pinkie at the exact midpoint of each string. These harmonics are the same pitch as the regular note in that place on the fingerboard, but the timbre is different.

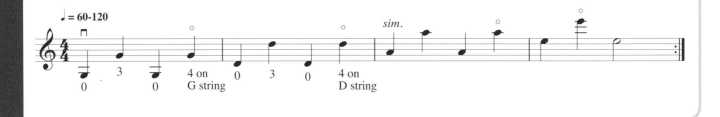

WED

Workout #234   **Rhythm Track:** #4   **Technique:** Rhythm/Feel   **Genre:** Swing/Blues

Description: This exercise forces you to swing and be accurate while playing at a number of dynamic levels. You've got to swing with double-stops, slurs, ghost notes, and big accents.

Tip: The parenthesized notes can be ghosted or swallowed. The etude is played in second position, but can be easily moved to play in a different key. It is an example of a box position that you can move around. If you're up for it, try playing this lick somewhere else.

THU

Workout #235   **Rhythm Track:** #2   **Technique:** Arpeggios   **Genre:** Any

Description: Today let's practice and compare four different chords. Using G as the root, we'll spell out the Gm(maj7), Gm7, Gm7♭5, and the Gdim7 chords.

Tip: Once this exercise makes sense, play these chord qualities using a different root. You may want to begin with a comfortable root like A and see how far you can go.

FRI

Workout #236   **Rhythm Track:** #4   **Technique:** Playing with Others   **Genre:** Swing/Jazz

Description: This is a short Circle of Fifths chord progression. Notice how the tritone of each dominant chord (the third and seventh degrees) descends chromatically. With these chords, we're also able to incorporate some open strings to fill out our comping.

Tip: Concentrate on the notes on the G and D strings, but add in the open A enough to add color to this chord progression.

SAT

Workout #237   **Rhythm Track:** #2   **Technique:** Bowing   **Genre:** Any pop style

Description: The written rhythm of this exercise is just like last week's, but this time we're going to do a tiny on-the-string retake between each note.

Tip: Playing all down-bows gives the articulation a certain sound and keeping the retakes on the string can add a subtle ghost note to the rhythm. You might have to practice getting enough bow back with your retakes so that you don't end up at the tip! Start slowly and make your retakes an audible part of the rhythm.

SUN

Workout #238   **Rhythm Track:** #1   **Technique:** Stretching Out   **Genre:** Pop

About the Example: Playing in 5/4 can seem intimidating at first, but listen to the recording and you'll be able to get this going pretty easily.

MON

Workout #239   **Rhythm Track:** #5   **Technique:** Scales   **Genre:** Any

Description: As its name suggests, the Lydian ♭7th scale is the Lydian scale with a ♭7th degree. Its pitches are derived from beginning on the fourth note of the melodic minor scale.

Tip: This is a cool scale to use to add spice when soloing over a held dominant chord. Fiddle players now and then use this scale in bluegrass for an interesting harmonic twist.

TUE

Workout #240   **Rhythm Track:** #2   **Technique:** Ornaments   **Genre:** Any pop style

Description: Let's put some double stops and grace notes together.

Tip: The grace notes and the open E string are played as a double stop right on the beat. Immediately lift your first finger while holding the open E. The recording will clear up any questions you might have.

WED

Workout #241   **Rhythm Track:** #2   **Technique:** Rhythm/Feel   **Genre:** Pop

Description: This exercise highlights two contrasting articulations, allowing you to practice alternating between them while staying rhythmic.

Tip: The 16th notes with the staccato dots should be short and percussive. The other notes need a little separation between them, but are much longer and more sustained. Carry your sound through those notes and give them a distinct, rhythmic ending.

THU

Workout #242   **Rhythm Track:** #2   **Technique:** Arpeggios   **Genre:** Any

Description: Like last week's exercise, this example spells out four different chord qualities with the same root. The chords are Amaj7, A6, A7, and A7#5.

Tip: Once you're comfortable with this exercise, play the notes of each chord in a different order – e.g., 1, 3, 5, 7 or 7, 5, 1, 3, etc. You can also practice transposing these chords to a different root.

FRI

Workout #243   **Rhythm Track:** #4   **Technique:** Playing with Others   **Genre:** Blues/Swing

Description: Let's forge a backing line by putting together two figures we've practiced previously.

Tip: Going back and forth between these two bow strokes requires you to alternate between chopping near the frog and playing the regular notes using a lot more bow.

SAT

Workout #244   **Rhythm Track:** #5   **Technique:** Bowing   **Genre:** Any

Description: Here's another exercise to isolate and improve your string crossings.

Tip: Stay economical with your bow. Make only as big a motion as you need. As you play this more quickly, your bow stroke will change from a forearm stroke to mostly a wrist motion.

SUN

Workout #245   **Rhythm Track:** #4   **Technique:** Stretching Out   **Genre:** Jazz

About the Example: This jazzy lick will give you a chance to put some of the scales you've practiced into a melodic context.

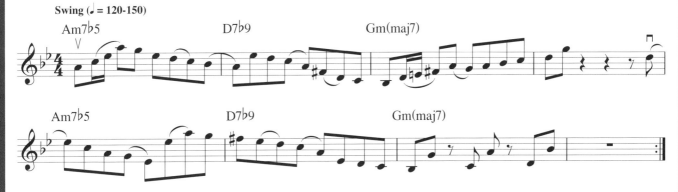

73

MON

Workout #246 **Rhythm Track:** #2 **Technique:** Scales **Genre:** Any

Description: This exercise will allow you to feel more comfortable – and play in tune! – as you perform in higher positions.

Tip: As you reach across the fingerboard, keep your fingers down as long as possible. This will help you develop a good hand frame as you work on playing in higher positions. As written, this exercise is played entirely in second position, but it could be transposed higher simply by beginning with your first finger on a higher note on the G string. Give it a try!

TUE

Workout #247 **Rhythm Track:** #4 **Technique:** Ornaments **Genre:** Any pop style

Description: For this exercise, we'll combine a few techniques into a big, dramatic wail.

Tip: The placement of the fingers for the rake across the lower three strings doesn't matter; you're only stopping the strings for the effect. Arrive on your pinkie, somewhere between the A and the B♭, on the downbeat. The grace notes in the fourth bar begin on the beat.

WED

Workout #248 **Rhythm Track:** #2 **Technique:** Rhythm/Feel **Genre:** Funk/Rock

Description: This exercise starts out with a cool-sounding triple stop. Make the 16ths that follow short and percussive.

Tip: The first group of 16ths starts down-bow on the "and" of the beat, the second is on an up-bow on the second 16th of the beat. Make sure both of these are rhythmically precise.

THU

Workout #249　　　　**Rhythm Track:** #2　　　　**Technique:** Arpeggios　　　　**Genre:** Any

Description: The min7♭5 chord shares its pitches with the minor 6th chord a minor third higher, in this case the Dm7♭5 and the Fmin6 chord.

Tip: With double-stop exercises like this one, the most demanding way to practice is to really sustain each pair of notes to the next. It's also fine to put some separation between the notes or to work on another articulation you'd like to practice.

FRI

Workout #250　　　　**Rhythm Track:** #3　　　　**Technique:** Playing with Others　　　　**Genre:** Any pop style

Description: To take a break (solo) in a song, a great starting point is to play the melody. In order to make it more interesting, you can embellish that melody.

Tip: This is a terrific way to begin improvising on the violin. Experiment with different bowings on this melody. Play it rubato, with expressive rhythmic freedom within an underlying tempo, and try shaping the melody different ways. You can also rearrange the ornaments or make up your own. As long as you keep the melody recognizable, you can do anything you want!

SAT

Workout #251　　　　**Rhythm Track:** #5　　　　**Technique:** Bowing　　　　**Genre:** Any

Description: Here's another exercise to work on your string crossings. It's easy to overdo the change in angle of the bow as you alternate between the two strings. Keep your movements as efficient as possible.

Tip: Make sure that the change of angle of the bow is only as great as you need. Play eighth notes with both pitches as a double stop, then gradually bring out the written pattern, adding only as much change of angle in the bow as is necessary to avoid the unplayed string.

SUN

Workout #252　　　　**Rhythm Track:** #2　　　　**Technique:** Stretching Out　　　　**Genre:** Blues/Roots

About the Example: Keep the eighth notes short and articulated. We're going for a decidedly rhythmic feel.

VIOLIN
AEROBICS

WEEK 37

MON

Workout #253 **Rhythm Track:** #2 **Technique:** Scales **Genre:** Any

Description: Chords made of fourths instead of thirds sound ambiguous; it's not obvious what key you're in. This is a cool sound that's common in many styles of jazz. Today's exercise gives you all the perfect fourths in first position.

Tip: You can also play this passage in reverse to practice descending fourths. If you're an advanced player, try creating some sequences of your own.

TUE

Workout #254 **Rhythm Track:** #2 **Technique:** Ornaments **Genre:** Any pop style

Description: In each measure of this exercise we'll play the same pitch twice, first normally and then as a harmonic.

Tip: All the harmonics in this exercise are played on the G string. Touch the string very lightly to sound each harmonic. In violin notation, Roman numerals correspond to the string to be played. IV is the G string, III is the D, and so on.

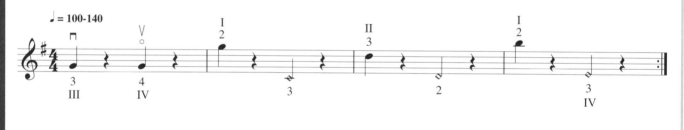

WED

Workout #255 **Rhythm Track:** #7 **Technique:** Rhythm/Feel **Genre:** Bluegrass

Description: Here's an up-tempo bluegrass lick in B minor. You'll be able to use some slides and work on getting a good feel.

Tip: Check out the recording for a sense of how this lick sounds. The notes with the half-step slides begin on the beat. Make sure the accents pop out; the other notes are less important.

THU

Workout #256 **Rhythm Track:** #2 **Technique:** Arpeggios **Genre:** Any

Description: Diminished 7th chords, like the augmented triads we've worked on, are an example of a symmetrical chord. There are only three distinct diminished 7th chords before the patterns repeat. Today's exercise allows us to practice D, F, G♯, and B diminished 7th chords. A bargain!

Tip: Most of the convenient double stops on the violin for this chord will be minor thirds, tritones, or major sixths. As you shift from one double stop to the next, you may want to use a different finger to play the same note in order to make the next pair of notes easier to play.

FRI

Workout #257 **Rhythm Track:** #5 **Technique:** Playing with Others **Genre:** Reggae

Description: Today we'll play a standard reggae figure. Reggae is a style of pop music developed in Jamaica, but its rhythms and sound have been incorporated into many styles and songs.

Tip: Take a listen to the recorded example – and some reggae albums! – to get a sense of this style. Bob Marley is probably the most famous reggae musician, but there are lots of artists to listen to. Play around with this pattern, accenting it in different ways.

SAT

Workout #258 **Rhythm Track:** #5 **Technique:** Bowing **Genre:** Irish

Description: Here's a rhythm to practice for precision and feel. The last two beats are a bit of a tongue twister.

Tip: Slowly practice the second half of the second bar (the last four notes) by itself. Once this feels comfortable, begin to increase the tempo, then play the complete exercise.

SUN

Workout #259 **Rhythm Track:** #4 **Technique:** Stretching Out **Genre:** Jazz

About the Example: Here's a jazzy lick in F. Keep your bowings smooth and swinging.

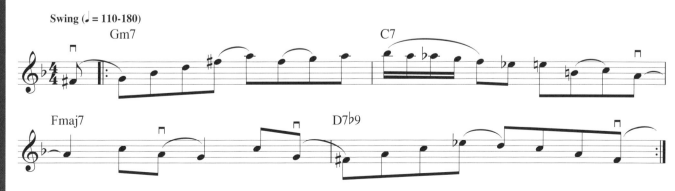

MON

Workout #260 **Rhythm Track:** #5 **Technique:** Scales **Genre:** Any

Description: This half-whole scale reverses the pattern of the whole-half diminished scale. This time you'll begin with the half-step and follow it with a whole step. This pattern repeats to create the scale.

Tip: This should feel familiar after learning the whole-half scale. This is a great scale to use with dominant ♭9 chords.

TUE

Workout #261 **Rhythm Track:** #3 **Technique:** Ornaments **Genre:** Any pop style

Description: Let's play the harmonics we've found so far on all four strings. The diamond notation indicates where your finger goes, not the pitch that results.

Tip: Play this in third position. If you have trouble sounding the harmonics, you can check the placement of your fingers by playing a stopped note in the same place, then lifting your finger almost off the string to sound the harmonic. A fast bow, an accent on each note, and bowing near the bridge can all help the harmonics to sound.

WED

Workout #262 **Rhythm Track:** #2 **Technique:** Rhythm/Feel **Genre:** Latin/Pop

Description: This exercise uses a cool D7#9 voicing in the first bar and will give you more practice with triple stops.

Tip: To sustain a three-note chord like this one, aim for the middle string. You'll need to use some extra weight in the arm to get all three strings to speak, so make sure to use a faster bow so the sound doesn't get too crunchy. Moving the bow away from the bridge and toward the fingerboard where the string angle is flatter will also help.

THU

Workout #263   **Rhythm Track:** #5   **Technique:** Arpeggios   **Genre:** Any

Description: Today's exercise is a cool-sounding pattern derived from the diminished scale. Getting comfortable with this etude will take you a long way toward becoming comfortable with the sound of this scale. This is terrific stuff to learn, but it isn't a common part of violin pedagogy.

Tip: Once you're comfortable with the exercise, see if you can play it starting on a different note. As always with the diminished scale, there are only three versions before you repeat the pattern.

FRI

Workout #264   **Rhythm Track:** #2   **Technique:** Playing with Others   **Genre:** Pop

Description: Let's play a rhythmic eighth-note figure with chords. This could work well as a backdrop in a pop song.

Tip: All this is played off the string, near the frog. Aim for the middle string with the bow. Stress the quarter-note pulse a bit to give the passage some weight.

SAT

Workout #265   **Rhythm Track:** #5   **Technique:** Bowing   **Genre:** Any

Description: Starting a bowing pattern on an up-bow can feel a little awkward at first, but in a triple meter like 6/8 or 12/8 it's the way to have a down-bow on the accents. This will make them easier to bring out.

Tip: Start slowly and highlight the accented notes on beats 2 and 4, the fourth and tenth eighth notes. Make sure your rhythm stays steady even as you make the string crossings.

SUN

Workout #266   **Rhythm Track:** #2   **Technique:** Stretching Out   **Genre:** Latin/Pop

About the Example: Today we'll turn some thirds and sixths into an interesting, syncopated rhythm.

MON

Workout #267 **Rhythm Track:** #5 **Technique:** Scales **Genre:** Any

Description: The Locrian natural 2 scale is derived from the melodic minor scale. It's the pattern of intervals created by beginning on the melodic minor's sixth degree.

Tip: The chord that's built by using this scale is a half-diminished, or min7♭5, chord. This is a tricky sounding name, but it's basically just the ii chord in a minor key. Because of that relationship, this scale works quite well with said chord.

TUE

Workout #268 **Rhythm Track:** #5 **Technique:** Ornaments **Genre:** Any pop style

Description: Today we'll learn to play "Reveille" (the "Wake up!" bugle call) using only harmonics. The first two bars teach you the finger pattern using regular notes; the second half uses the same pattern with harmonics to play the tune.

Tip: All the notes are played on the G string in third position. Find the harmonics before you play the example. The stopped C becomes a high-pitched G, the D becomes a higher-octave D, and the E becomes a high-pitched B.

WED

Workout #269 **Rhythm Track:** #5 **Technique:** Rhythm/Feel **Genre:** Pop

Description: This is an interesting excerpt for its rhythm and for the contrast between the dissimilar bow strokes.

Tip: The first pair of notes should be a quick gesture at the frog. The other, longer notes should start in the upper half. A slight retake between the two up-bows might help you get the right feel.

THU

Workout #270 **Rhythm Track:** #5 **Technique:** Arpeggios **Genre:** Any

Description: There are only four arpeggios for augmented triads. Because of the symmetry of the scale, once you've played the first four chromatic possibilities, you begin repeating the triads you've already outlined. This exercise puts all the possibilities in first position, and a bit beyond, into four bars.

Tip: The augmented fifths created by every other note of this pattern are tricky to play on the violin. Go slowly and be patient. Happily, there are really only four arpeggios to learn!

FRI

Workout #271 **Rhythm Track:** #4 **Technique:** Playing with Others **Genre:** Jazz

Description: Let's get some practice with comping at a slower tempo.

Tip: There should be some separation between the quarter notes, but they're still pretty long and smooth. Put a bit of an accent on beats 2 and 4.

SAT

Workout #272 **Rhythm Track:** #2 **Technique:** Bowing **Genre:** Any

Description: Players with a classical background will recognize this famous string-crossing pattern from J.S. Bach's E major partita.

Tip: This is a tricky bowing. Practice it slowly at first and keep your string crossings clean and precise. Feeling an accent on each beat may help.

SUN

Workout #273 **Rhythm Track:** #2 **Technique:** Stretching Out **Genre:** Funk

About the Example: Play this lick at the frog with a percussive, vertical bow stroke. Subdivide the beat in your head and stay precise.

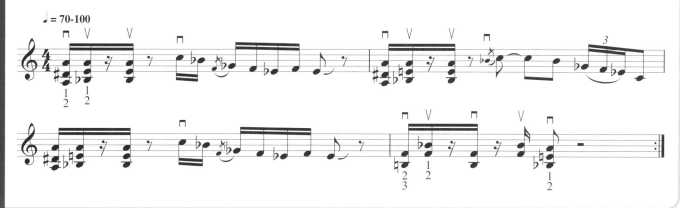

WEEK 40

MON

Workout #274   **Rhythm Track:** #2   **Technique:** Scales   **Genre:** Any

Description: Today we'll get more comfortable with the Locrian natural 2 scale by playing the 7th chords created by the scale. We'll use a root of B. These are pitches that work well with a Bmin7♭5 (B half-diminished) chord.

Tip: Think about the relationship between the degrees of the scale as you play this. The order of the chord degrees in this exercise is 5, 3, 1, 7. Try playing these 7th chords using a different pattern, e.g., 7, 5, 3, 1 or 5, 1, 3, 7, etc.

TUE

Workout #275   **Rhythm Track:** #5   **Technique:** Ornaments   **Genre:** Any pop style

Description: Pizzicato can work well played in guitar position with your thumb. Let's try it!

Tip: Get a good bit of flesh on the string and give it a strong pull for a big, full sound. It may take a bit of practice to do this quickly.

WED

Workout #276   **Rhythm Track:** #4   **Technique:** Rhythm/Feel   **Genre:** Jazz

Description: Today's excerpt is a jazzy bebop lick. Bebop is a subgenre of jazz made famous by saxophonist Charlie Parker and trumpeter Dizzy Gillespie in the 1950s.

Tip: Listen to the recording to get a sense of the lick. If this style appeals to you, check out some recordings by the guys listed above. Jean-Luc Ponty incorporated a lot of this kind of playing into his early recordings. It's amazing to hear!

THU

Workout #277   **Rhythm Track:** #5   **Technique:** Arpeggios   **Genre:** Any

Description: Today we'll play an A7#5 arpeggio. We're adding a seventh to the #5 (augmented) arpeggios that we've previously practiced. On this chord, the #5 is E♯. This is the correct spelling of this pitch, but it is enharmonic (the same sound spelled differently) to an F♮.

Tip: The pitches in the exercise spell an A augmented 7th chord, but we'll finger the E♯ as we would an F♮. It can be frustrating at first to see these odd notes (C♭, F♭, etc.), but they exist for a reason and you'll soon be able to see past their awkward-seeming use.

FRI

Workout #278   **Rhythm Track:** #2   **Technique:** Playing with Others   **Genre:** Latin

Description: A "montuno" is a rhythmic vamp that is common in Latin music. This example will probably sound familiar and is great fun to play.

Tip: Keep the notes very short. Instead of sustaining the notes, use a vertical, off-the-string bowing. Listening to the recording will help you. This lick also sounds great played pizzicato.

SAT

Workout #279   **Rhythm Track:** #7   **Technique:** Bowing   **Genre:** Any pop style

Description: Here's an awkward little passage that's good practice for your bow arm.

Tip: Play this exercise in the lower half of the bow. Pay attention to how much bow you're using for the slurs vs. the separate notes.

SUN

Workout #280   **Rhythm Track:** #4   **Technique:** Stretching Out   **Genre:** Jazz

About the Example: This melody over a ii-V-I progression in C uses the altered chord and scale. We'll learn more about them soon.

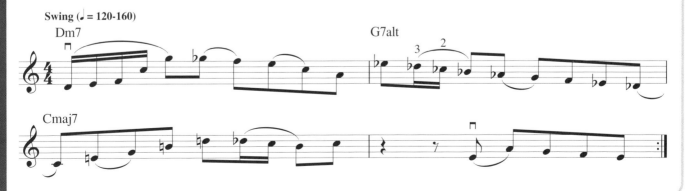

MON

Workout #281 **Rhythm Track:** #5 **Technique:** Scales **Genre:** Any
Description: This exercise will help you become more facile with the whole tone scale.
Tip: Once you're comfortable with this scale, try playing it a half step higher. This will give you some more practice on the other version – there are only two – of the whole tone scale.

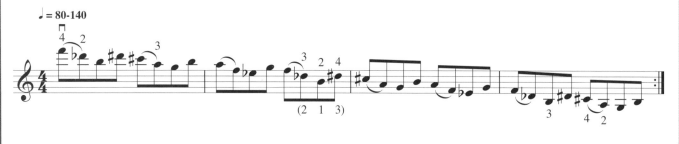

TUE

Workout #282 **Rhythm Track:** #7 **Technique:** Ornaments **Genre:** Any pop style
Description: Let's try a strummed rhythmic pattern. We're not trying to play any pitches, we just want rhythm.
Tip: Hold the violin in guitar position and lightly dampen the strings with the fingers of your left hand. Touch the tips of your thumb and index finger together. You can use the nails of those two fingers to strum the string. Follow the up and down directions for your strums; "down" is toward the E string, "up" is toward your head.

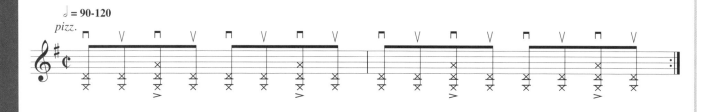

WED

Workout #283 **Rhythm Track:** #2 **Technique:** Rhythm/Feel **Genre:** Funk/Pop
Description: This is an excellent exercise to work on your rhythmic evenness. It also forces you to be consistent when the bowing reverses.
Tip: Play all the separate notes off the string and keep them perfectly even. Pay attention to the separate notes immediately after the slur to make sure that you're steady as the bowing reverses.

THU

Workout #284   **Rhythm Track:** #5   **Technique:** Arpeggios   **Genre:** Any

Description: Today we'll spell out a G7 chord and play it as an arpeggio. Chords written with only a note name and a "7" are called dominant chords. They are derived from the chord built on the fifth note (dominant) of a major scale. We've had a lot of dominant chord practice, so try cranking up the tempo on this one!

Tip: The interval between the third (B, in this example) and the seventh (F) of a dominant chord is a tritone. This interval requires a little extra attention on the violin. Try both printed fingerings. The main fingering will be smoother and easier to play in tune, but sometimes you'll need to use the "hopping" fingering.

FRI

Workout #285   **Rhythm Track:** #5   **Technique:** Playing with Others   **Genre:** Reggae

Description: Let's use our reggae riff from Week 37 and fill it out with a half-time chop.

Tip: All of this is played at the frog. On the pitched notes, the bow should come off the string immediately so the strings can ring briefly; then lift your left-hand fingers to end the note. Catch your open E string on the chords for an even bigger sound.

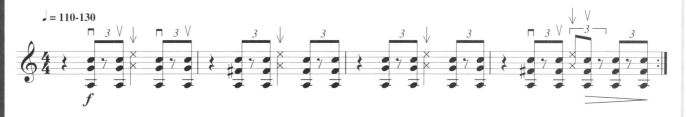

SAT

Workout #286   **Rhythm Track:** #5   **Technique:** Bowing   **Genre:** Any

Description: Today's etude is terrific for your bow arm. This bowing is surprisingly useful in smaller chunks, too. The articulation that comes from stopping the bow on the string is just like what we're going for in some of the pop styles we're studying.

Tip: Keep the bow on the string for the eighth notes. If you've played this bowing in your classical repertoire, you may want to dig in just a touch more. This stroke sounds most convincing in the middle and lower half of the bow.

SUN

Workout #287   **Rhythm Track:** #2   **Technique:** Stretching Out   **Genre:** Jazz/Rock

About the Example: This exercise combines the C Dorian and G whole tone scales into a short riff and melody.

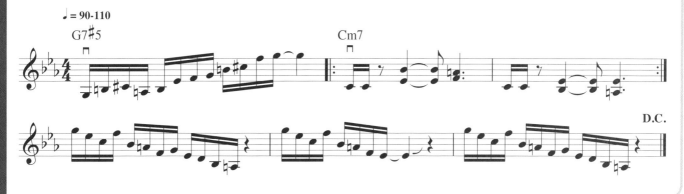

MON

Workout #288   **Rhythm Track:** #2   **Technique:** Scales   **Genre:** Any
Description: Keep your fingers down throughout this exercise. The goal is to be able to move up the fingerboard with a consistent hand frame.
Tip: Try this with a drone on A and be demanding with yourself about intonation. Keep your left hand relaxed and use only the pressure necessary to sound the notes.

TUE

Workout #289   **Rhythm Track:** #7   **Technique:** Ornaments   **Genre:** Any pop style
Description: Let's try an unpitched rhythmic figure to explore some more strumming techniques.
Tip: Hold your violin in guitar position. Bring out the accents on the upbeats. The up-stroke eighth notes can be quieter than the other notes. You can use just your thumb, or touch your thumb and index finger together and use your nails to strum the strings.

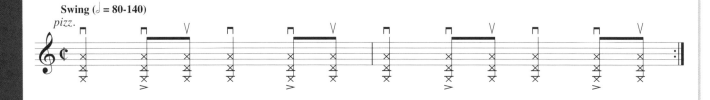

WED

Workout #290   **Rhythm Track:** #2   **Technique:** Rhythm/Feel   **Genre:** Any
Description: A repeating pattern of three 16th notes over a foundation of four 16th notes is a common syncopation in popular music. This figure has a string crossing that reverses direction each time. If you enjoy this sound, check out some rags.
Tip: Keep your string crossings compact and efficient. Change the angle of the bow only as much as is necessary to clear the unplayed string.

THU

Workout #291 **Rhythm Track:** #5 **Technique:** Arpeggios **Genre:** Any

Description: It's uncommon to practice the min7♭5 arpeggio in traditional violin pedagogy, but it is a common chord in jazz. This exercise outlines a Bmin7♭5 chord. This sonority is often called a half-diminished chord, but is exactly the same.

Tip: The tritone (six half steps) created by the ♭5th can make intonation a little tricky. Pay attention to this interval as you practice the exercise.

FRI

Workout #292 **Rhythm Track:** #2 **Technique:** Playing with Others **Genre:** Funk/Pop

Description: Here's a funky riff that would work well behind another player or singer.

Tip: Keep the chopped notes in the background and bring out the pitched figure. You can play this straight or slightly swung.

SAT

Workout #293 **Rhythm Track:** #2 **Technique:** Bowing **Genre:** Any

Description: This is a fun bowing and can be a great device for playing solo. By playing chords with your left hand, you can create a harmonic backdrop. Or, use it in a solo. It looks flashy and audiences love it.

Tip: This is a three-string version of the bowing exercise we did in the first week of the book (page 5). Put a tiny accent on each bow to keep your string crossings rhythmic. Once you've got the hang of this, try to think of each three (or six) notes as a gesture, but keep your ear on the metronome so the tail doesn't wag the dog!

SUN

Workout #294 **Rhythm Track:** #2 **Technique:** Stretching Out **Genre:** Funk

About the Example: This funk riff in B minor puts double and triple stops together with a number of the bowings and articulations that we've studied.

MON

Workout #295   **Rhythm Track:** #5   **Technique:** Scales   **Genre:** Any
Description: This exercise is a simple sequence using the whole tone scale. This reordering of the pitches will help you get more comfortable with it.
Tip: Play this scale backward to become accustomed to descending by whole steps as well. Be open to using a different fingering on the way down than you did on the way up.

TUE

Workout #296   **Rhythm Track:** #2   **Technique:** Ornaments   **Genre:** Any pop style
Description: "Aha!" you say. "Pizzicato with a slur?" Yep. Let's try it.
Tip: Rake your thumb across the string in rhythm. It will take a bit of practice to make it rhythmic. The "plus" above the open E string is the symbol used to indicate left-hand pizzicato on the violin. Keep your third finger down as you play the A, then pluck the open string with that finger.

WED

Workout #297   **Rhythm Track:** #1   **Technique:** Rhythm/Feel   **Genre:** Rock
Description: Here's a good exercise to practice changing time signatures. This example alternates between 4/4 and 3/4, but you might see a similar passage written as 7/4.
Tip: This looks a little daunting, but is actually straightforward to play. Just keep counting quarter-note beats and pay attention to the changes in feel.

THU

Workout #298   **Rhythm Track:** #2   **Technique:** Arpeggios   **Genre:** Any

Description: This week we'll go a little farther up the fingerboard on an Fm7 chord.

Tip: Use a drone on F to keep your intonation honest. Try playing the high minor seventh in fourth position using your second and fourth fingers.

FRI

Workout #299   **Rhythm Track:** #5   **Technique:** Playing with Others   **Genre:** Swing

Description: Playing all the quarter-note pulses with down-strokes makes it easy to add in some rhythmic accents on the "and" of the beat with an up-stroke.

Tip: Hold your violin in guitar position. Use your thumbnail to play these off-beat eighth-note accents.

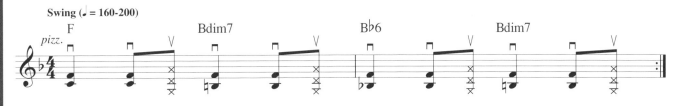

SAT

Workout #300   **Rhythm Track:** #2   **Technique:** Bowing   **Genre:** Any

Description: This exercise is similar to last week's, but with four notes per beat. It's a very quick version of the bowing we played in our first week.

Tip: Make sure to catch the E string on the up-bow to help solidify your rhythm. We want all four notes to be distinctly heard.

SUN

Workout #301   **Rhythm Track:** #2   **Technique:** Stretching Out   **Genre:** Latin/Jazz

About the Example: Aim for a flowing, lyrical sound with this example. We're using the i, ii, and V chords in E minor.

MON

Workout #302   **Rhythm Track:** #5   **Technique:** Scales   **Genre:** Any

Description: Here's another blues scale using our "box" concept. By employing a familiar hand shape and no open strings, we can move licks or play in tricky keys more easily.

Tip: This is an example similar to the one we played in Week 16 (page 34). This time we'll play two octaves. Try reversing the example to practice descending down the scale.

TUE

Workout #303   **Rhythm Track:** #5   **Technique:** Ornaments   **Genre:** Any pop style

Description: A cool effect we're going to try today is singing in unison with what we're playing. This can be a neat sound and can also give you ideas for your playing.

Tip: Play the first two bars to get the notes in your ear. Next sing that same short scale on "loo," or a syllable of your choosing. It's fine if you need to sing the phrase in a different octave. Finally, put the playing and singing together and see what you think.

WED

Workout #304   **Rhythm Track:** #2   **Technique:** Rhythm/Feel   **Genre:** Rock

Description: Here's an exercise to practice your syncopated up-bows. This is a rock riff, so go for a rhythmic, aggressive sound.

Tip: You'll have to concentrate in order to be precise with the rhythm that alternates between playing on and off the beat. Try dampening the strings with your left hand on the rests to get a more intense rhythmic feel. It's fine to hear the retakes. Tune in to the sound of the click so that all those up-bows stay in time.

THU

Workout #305 Rhythm Track: #5 Technique: Arpeggios Genre: Any

Description: In minor keys, it's common for the V7 (pronounced "five-seven") chord to have a ♭9. For example, in C minor you might play a G7♭9 chord. This chord adds the ninth, the same pitch as the second note of the scale, to a dominant chord and lowers that note by a half step. In the case of our A7♭9 example, the ♭9 is B♭.

Tip: Try several fingerings for this exercise. Depending on the lick you're playing, you might want to use a different finger for the same pitch at different times. This chord will often resolve to D minor. Try playing a different V7♭9 chord. It will be like the dominant chords we've already looked at, but with an extra note a half step above the root.

FRI

Workout #306 Rhythm Track: #5 Technique: Playing with Others Genre: Jazz/Swing

Description: Let's play a jazzy vamp with quickly changing chords and some eighth-note embellishments.

Tip: At first, you might find this tricky to play. To begin, try leaving out the eighth notes on the "ands" of the beat. When this is comfortable, bring out the accents and add in the eighth notes. With a little practice, you'll get there!

SAT

Workout #307 Rhythm Track: #5 Technique: Bowing Genre: Funk

Description: Let's use the up-bow and down-bow staccato that we've worked on and apply it to a simple lick.

Tip: Go slowly at first. The articulation is the most important part of this exercise. With this bow stroke, many of the articulations we're shooting for become almost automatic.

SUN

Workout #308 Rhythm Track: #2 Technique: Stretching Out Genre: Pop

About the Example: Catch the E string on the up-bow for a tiny accent to keep the rhythm precise. Experiment with differing dynamics to turn this exercise into a short musical statement.

MON

Workout #309   **Rhythm Track:** #5   **Technique:** Scales   **Genre:** Any

Description: Because of the construction of the whole tone scale, there are really only two scales to learn. On the violin, one scale begins on the lowest G, the other on A♭. After that, the notes repeat. Playing in a different key is just a matter of playing the pitches you've already practiced, but beginning on a different note.

Tip: One trick to playing the whole tone scale well is being able to make the change from what, on the violin, often feels like flat notes to what feels like sharped notes. Don't marry your fingerings to how the note is spelled. Another thing to be aware of is the leap from, say, a high third finger to a low first finger as you ascend. Try different fingerings so that you'll be ready for whatever comes your way.

TUE

Workout #310   **Rhythm Track:** #4   **Technique:** Ornaments   **Genre:** Any pop style

Description: Let's put some unison singing into a riff.

Tip: You might want to approach this like we did last week. Play it first to get the notes in your ear, then sing the same figure before combining the playing and singing. If your voice feels more comfortable singing the line in a different octave, that's fine. You'll have to do an on-the-string retake between the down-bows. You can let the retake sound a little bit for some extra feel.

WED

Workout #311   **Rhythm Track:** #1   **Technique:** Rhythm/Feel   **Genre:** Pop

Description: Here's an example in 7/8 to get yourself more comfortable with less common time signatures.

Tip: When a riff fills out the bars without rests like this, it's easier to count. Try leaving out the last four notes of each bar and resting until the next downbeat to further internalize this time signature.

Workout #312 **Rhythm Track:** #2 **Technique:** Arpeggios **Genre:** Any

Description: Raising the fifth of a dominant chord to create a V7#5 is a common alteration. You might see the chord we're playing today written as G7+5 (the plus symbol is sometimes use to indicate a sharp), G7#5, or Gaug7.

Tip: It can be easier to play the D# of this exercise when you recognize that it's enharmonic to E♭. The fingerings given reflect that idea.

Workout #313 **Rhythm Track:** #2 **Technique:** Playing with Others **Genre:** Funk

Description: Here's a dominant #9 chord going to a little riff over D7 in the second bar. This riff is something you might play in a funk tune. (The #9 of an A7 is correctly spelled B#, but is written here enharmonically as C.)

Tip: Think of a funk band with horns kicking off a tune. (Check out Maceo Parker!) Give a good accent to the notes in the first bar. Play near the frog with an aggressive, off-the-string stroke. Aim for the middle string of the triple stop.

Workout #314 **Rhythm Track:** #5 **Technique:** Bowing **Genre:** Jazz/Latin

Description: This is an Afro-Cuban rhythm that will give your bow arm – and your mind! – a good workout.

Tip: Stay focused on your metronome as you play. This can be a tricky rhythm at first, so begin very slowly and increase the tempo only as you become more confident.

Workout #315 **Rhythm Track:** #2 **Technique:** Stretching Out **Genre:** Funk/Blues

About the Example: Concentrate on keeping your rhythm precise and grooving as you alternate between several different bow strokes.

MON

Workout #316   **Rhythm Track:** #5   **Technique:** Scales   **Genre:** Any

Description: The Locrian natural 2 scale is derived from the melodic minor scale. It's the pattern of intervals created by starting on the melodic minor scale's sixth note. This scale is useful for playing over min7♭5 (half-diminished) chords. It also can be thought of as a Locrian scale with a raised second note. (Locrian is the scale pattern that results from starting a major scale on its seventh note.)

Tip: Playing in half position is always a little tricky, especially that G♭ on the E string. Go slowly at first for intonation and use a C drone on your tuner to keep yourself honest.

TUE

Workout #317   **Rhythm Track:** #2   **Technique:** Ornaments   **Genre:** Any pop style

Description: It's possible to play many more harmonics than those we've explored on the open strings. By using your first finger to basically create an artificial nut, we can take the harmonic from the first measure and move it higher.

Tip: The bottom pitch is played solidly with your first finger. The upper (diamond) pitch is played very lightly with your pinkie. Each bar contains one pitch played two ways: first as regular note, then as a harmonic.

WED

Workout #318   **Rhythm Track:** #7   **Technique:** Rhythm/Feel   **Genre:** Any

Description: This rhythmic change, between duple and triple figures, is something that always takes an extra bit of attention to do well. This exercise removes any other elements so you can focus on the concept.

Tip: Pay close attention to your metronome. Arriving precisely at the second beat of each bar is what we're after. That's the point at which any imprecision is most evident.

THU

Workout #319   **Rhythm Track:** #5   **Technique:** Arpeggios   **Genre:** Any

Description: Here's another chance to get your m7♭5 chord (half diminished) playing together. Today we'll play an Fm7♭5. This is a tricky chord that will often show up in tunes in E♭ minor, which occur more frequently in jazz than a violinist might like!

Tip: The ♭5th is correctly written as C♭, but as a violinist you may feel more comfortable thinking of fingering it as a B as you play this.

FRI

Workout #320   **Rhythm Track:** #2   **Technique:** Playing with Others   **Genre:** Pop

Description: It can really fill out an accompaniment to add a third note to the double stops we've been playing. Of course, this isn't always feasible or practical, but in certain keys or on particular chords it can be pretty easy to do.

Tip: Unless the string angle of your bridge is pretty flat, sustaining three strings at once is possible only when you're really wailing away. But a lot of pop music allows you to play pretty loudly, so this can still work.

SAT

Workout #321   **Rhythm Track:** #5   **Technique:** Bowing   **Genre:** Irish

Description: This figure is common in Irish fiddling. It's one of that style's basic rhythms and is a good one to practice.

Tip: Once you feel comfortable with this, try playing the 16th notes very late and very quickly – like an ornament rather than a measured rhythm. If you dig into the string and choke it just a bit, you'll start to develop a common Irish ornament sometimes referred to as a "treble."

SUN

Workout #322   **Rhythm Track:** #4   **Technique:** Stretching Out   **Genre:** Jazz

About the Example: When you're confident with the notes, find ways to make the passage expressive using accents and dynamics. Try using other bowings as well.

MON

Workout #323 **Rhythm Track:** #5 **Technique:** Scales **Genre:** Any

Description: The altered scale takes its name from the fact that basically every note that can be altered, is. Build the scale by beginning with the essential notes of a dominant chord (the 1, 3, and ♭7) and add the ♭9, #9, #11, and ♭13. (To make this introduction easier, some of these notes are spelled enharmonically here.) It's a mouthful to say, but this is a common chord in jazz; knowing this scale will make things easy.

Tip: Here is yet another scale derived from the melodic minor, this time by beginning on the melodic minor's seventh degree. This scale can sound great over a dominant chord that is about to resolve to its tonic. Because of this scale's relationship to the melodic minor scale, playing this may already feel familiar.

TUE

Workout #324 **Rhythm Track:** #2 **Technique:** Ornaments **Genre:** Any pop style

Description: Now let's expand on last week's exercise by playing a scale made up entirely of harmonics. The pitches in this exercise will sound two octaves above the fully stopped note, either the nut of the violin or the first finger.

Tip: This exercise uses the first and fourth fingers together to play most of the harmonics, so we'll be doing a lot of shifting.

WED

Workout #325 **Rhythm Track:** Exercise #325 **Technique:** Rhythm/Feel **Genre:** Any

Description: Here's an interesting exercise that we're going to do without the violin. Clap the written rhythm along with the track on the recording. During the rests, the click will drop out. When you clap the downbeat of bars 3 and 6, see if you're perfectly with the click.

Tip: During breaks in the music, when the rhythm section stops playing, it's common for everyone's time to be slightly different. (The arrival on the next downbeat isn't always pretty!) Practice this exercise so you can learn to keep a perfectly even pulse. As an additional exercise, try this with a friend. Both of you should close your eyes so that you don't have any clues as to where the other person is in their counting. See if you can both arrive on the downbeat exactly together. It's difficult to do, but excellent practice!

THU

Workout #326   **Rhythm Track:** #5   **Technique:** Arpeggios   **Genre:** Any

Description: Today's exercise uses a chord you often hear in "gypsy jazz" tunes. It's also the signature "private eye" chord. The minor chord with a major seventh (referred to as a minor/major 7th chord) works well with the melodic minor scale.

Tip: The quirky part of playing this chord is the augmented fifth between the third and seventh (in this case, Db and A, respectively) of the chord. Try getting used to several fingerings so that you'll be comfortable with any passage or with improvising on this chord.

FRI

Workout #327   **Rhythm Track:** #5   **Technique:** Playing with Others   **Genre:** Irish

Description: By putting together our double stop and rhythmic exercises, we can come up with an accompaniment figure for a jig.

Tip: Bring out the offset accents to give this example more interest.

SAT

Workout #328   **Rhythm Track:** #7   **Technique:** Bowing   **Genre:** Country/Pop

Description: This pattern of string crossings is called a "triple shuffle" and is used in the well-known tune "Orange Blossom Special." This excerpt uses different pitches, but the bowing is the same.

Tip: If you're having trouble, ignore the left hand and play the pattern on open strings.

SUN

Workout #329   **Rhythm Track:** #4   **Technique:** Stretching Out   **Genre:** Blues/Swing

About the Example: Swing hard as you combine into this joyous 12 bars a number of the techniques we've studied.

MON

Workout #330   **Rhythm Track:** #5   **Technique:** Scales   **Genre:** Any

Description: Today we'll expand our comfort with the altered scale. We'll play the 7th chords that are created by using the scale with a root of B♭. These are notes that would work well with a B♭ alt. chord. Some of the pitches are spelled enharmonically; pay attention to the sound.

Tip: This version of the melodic minor can be difficult to play by ear. By putting the scale into a series of sequences, you'll jumpstart your ability to really hear this scale. Once you have a sense of this exercise, play it in a different key.

TUE

Workout #331   **Rhythm Track:** #2   **Technique:** Ornaments   **Genre:** Any pop style

Description: This exercise mimics a guitar technique in which the guitarist plays two notes and bends the lower pitch up to a unison. It's a neat effect that can add variety to your playing.

Tip: The first two bars isolate the upper string of the lick. Once you feel comfortable with these shifts, add in the lower string. You're looking for a sweep up to the unison. This extension with your pinkie is much easier if you bring your left elbow around under the violin.

WED

Workout #332   **Rhythm Track:** #1   **Technique:** Rhythm/Feel   **Genre:** Rock

Description: Playing in "odd-time" meters like 5/4 or 7/8 can be a nice change from 4/4, but it's tough to internalize at first. Here's a riff to practice in 7/8. If you enjoy odd-meter tunes, you need to check out Jerry Goodman!

Tip: Practice these two measures with your metronome ticking eighth notes. Once you've got the hang of this, play it with a quarter-note click. Every other time through the riff, the click will move from on the beat to off the beat and back again.

THU

Workout #333 **Rhythm Track:** #2 **Technique:** Arpeggios **Genre:** Any

Description: Since diminished 7th chords are symmetrical, this exercise's root could be A, C, E♭, or F♯. There are only three unique diminished 7th chords. After that, the pitches will repeat themselves.

Tip: As you work through the pattern, you may find that you're more comfortable if you play some of the same pitches with a different finger at different times. Experiment with different fingerings to see what works well for you.

FRI

Workout #334 **Rhythm Track:** #2 **Technique:** Playing with Others **Genre:** Any pop style

Description: We can perform some licks that otherwise wouldn't be possible – and wow the audience! – if we play double stops and, at the same time, sing a third pitch to form chords. Check it out.

Tip: Begin by singing the notes in the first two bars. Then play the next two bars so that they're automatic. Finally, sing the first part and play the second part at the same time. It's tricky, but it's cool!

SAT

Workout #335 **Rhythm Track:** #5 **Technique:** Bowing **Genre:** Any

Description: Here's a flashy bowing that's fun to play. At a quick tempo it can really shine.

Tip: Start up-bow and catch the string so you can get it to bounce a bit, then feel the weight in your arm throughout the slurred notes. See how far you can raise the tempo on this one.

SUN

Workout #336 **Rhythm Track:** #2 **Technique:** Stretching Out **Genre:** Blues/Pop

About the Example: Let's put our octave preparation to good use! Put most of the stress on the lower note to help the octaves sound full and in tune.

M O N

Workout #337 **Rhythm Track:** #5 **Technique:** Scales **Genre:** Any
Description: This exercise uses the whole tone scale descending in a pattern of thirds. Some notes are spelled enharmonically.
Tip: Try playing this exercise in reverse to practice ascending on these pitches.

T U E

Workout #338 **Rhythm Track:** #2 **Technique:** Ornaments **Genre:** Any pop style
Description: We can use vibrato on our fingered harmonics!
Tip: To get comfortable with this, play the note without vibrato to find the right pressure and distance between your fingers so that the harmonic sounds. Then add a wide vibrato by moving your whole hand slightly to move the pitch.

W E D

Workout #339 **Rhythm Track:** #7 **Technique:** Rhythm/Feel **Genre:** Any
Description: The exercises for Weeks 49 and 50 show you an extremely effective way to practice a fast passage made up of constant eighth or 16th notes.
Tip: The first bar of this exercise is an example of a passage you want to learn to play quickly. Each of the measures that follow is a way to practice that passage. Start slowly and keep increasing the tempo to push yourself. Once you've played the figure each of those three ways for a while, the original eighth-note figure will be much smoother and easier.

THU

Workout #340   **Rhythm Track:** #5   **Technique:** Arpeggios   **Genre:** Any

Description: If we play the triads created by the whole tone scale, we get a series of augmented triads, each one a whole step above the previous one. This is a tricky pattern on the violin, but it sounds cool and is a useful exercise.

Tip: Because of the symmetry of the whole tone scale, there are only two possibilities for this exercise. Once you've conquered this etude, play it a half step higher. When you've done that, you've tackled all the augmented triads.

FRI

Workout #341   **Rhythm Track:** #2   **Technique:** Playing with Others   **Genre:** Any pop style

Description: Strummed pizzicato rhythm figures like this one allow you to change up the role that the violin plays in a group and add variety to your playing.

Tip: Hold your violin like a guitar. Touch your right index finger and thumb together. Use your nails to strum the strings. Bring out the pitched notes. Play the unpitched notes – those with an x for a note head – by releasing the pressure in the left-hand fingers, but keeping them in contact with the string.

SAT

Workout #342   **Rhythm Track:** #7   **Technique:** Bowing   **Genre:** Irish

Description: Here's a fun exercise to give your bow arm a workout.

Tip: Go for a lively sound. Don't worry about holding the quarter notes for their full value.

SUN

Workout #343   **Rhythm Track:** #2   **Technique:** Stretching Out   **Genre:** Blues

About the Example: We'll combine our box concept in second position with some open As to create this short, hip riff.

MON

Workout #344   **Rhythm Track:** #1   **Technique:** Scales   **Genre:** Any

Description: Playing double stops is a great way to internalize a scale, and playing them all the way up one string is an excellent way to develop your hand frame and shifting. Today we'll be using the A melodic minor scale.

Tip: This is a tricky exercise if you haven't been playing for very long. If you're able to play this right off, terrific! If you're not completely comfortable with something like this, go slowly. Remember to bring your elbow around under the violin and be careful to keep your intonation honest.

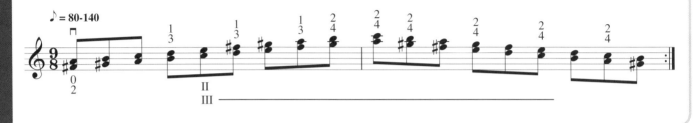

TUE

Workout #345   **Rhythm Track:** #7   **Technique:** Ornaments   **Genre:** Any pop style

Description: Let's try chopping in a triple meter.

Tip: Play the chops on beats 2 and 4 on higher strings to help bring out the accent and mimic a drumbeat. When you dampen the strings or the chops, the exact placement of your fingers isn't important. We're just going for an unpitched, rhythmic sound.

WED

Workout #346   **Rhythm Track:** #1   **Technique:** Rhythm/Feel   **Genre:** Any

Description: This week's exercise is a continuation from last week.

Tip: Using the one-measure example from the beginning of last week's exercise, here are four more rhythms to build your speed and cleanliness. As with any tricky passage, start slowly, use your metronome, and gradually increase the tempo.

THU

Workout #347 **Rhythm Track:** #5 **Technique:** Arpeggios **Genre:** Any
Description: Here's another m7♭5 arpeggio, this time on E. Today's Em7♭5 might show up as the "ii" chord in D minor.
Tip: Once you're comfortable with this exercise, see if you can add an A7♭9 for a bar or two, then end on a D minor arpeggio. Such a progression is extremely common in minor-key jazz tunes.

FRI

Workout #348 **Rhythm Track:** #4 **Technique:** Playing with Others **Genre:** Any pop style
Description: When it comes time to take a solo, a great way to get everyone's attention is to play it pizzicato. Audiences love it!
Tip: Play everything with your thumb while holding the violin in guitar position. It might take a little practice to get your thumb to move quickly enough, but it's an excellent way to get pizzes to really pop out.

SAT

Workout #349 **Rhythm Track:** #5 **Technique:** Bowing **Genre:** Irish
Description: Here's a great exercise for working on your bowing. There are two bowings to try with this exercise, one written above the staff, the other below.
Tip: Be sure to use your metronome and keep focusing on it. Stay as relaxed as you can. Both these bowings can be difficult to do for very long at a fast tempo!

SUN

Workout #350 **Rhythm Track:** #7 **Technique:** Stretching Out **Genre:** Bluegrass
About the Example: This short bluegrass tune uses a Lydian ♭7 scale for some harmonic interest.

103

MON

Workout #351 **Rhythm Track:** #1 **Technique:** Scales **Genre:** Any

Description: There are countless ways to practice scales. When you'd like to develop more fluency with a scale or key, find as many methods as you can to approach the material. You'll keep your practice interesting and develop your technique more quickly. Today we'll play a major scale with sevenths.

Tip: As you move through this etude, think about the interval of the next double stop before you play it. If you're having trouble, sound the bottom note of each pair first and then add the upper pitch. Once you're comfortable with this exercise, practice it in a different key or try playing sevenths using a more exotic scale.

TUE

Workout #352 **Rhythm Track:** #2 **Technique:** Ornaments **Genre:** Any pop style

Description: A cool effect that sounds a bit like electric guitar feedback can be created with harmonics, but will take some practice. A wide vibrato on the harmonic can further the illusion.

Tip: The two notes will be in the same place on the fingerboard, but the harmonic will require more finger pressure than the other harmonics we've played. Use the very tip of your finger, or even your fingernail, for the harmonic. A slow, heavy bow stroke near the bridge will help, too.

WED

Workout #353 **Rhythm Track:** #4 **Technique:** Rhythm/Feel **Genre:** Any pop style

Description: The point of this simplest looking of exercises is to give you a chance to experiment with *where* you put the notes. (The actual idea is *when* you play the notes, but this is sometimes referred to as *where* you play them.)

Tip: In popular music, great players have a well-developed sense of timing and are able to change feels and communicate tension or relaxation in part by making small adjustments to when they play a note. Practice this exercise in three different ways: 1) play each note precisely with your metronome; 2) play each note slightly before each click; 3) play each note slightly after each click. See what each of these feels and sounds like.

THU

Workout #354 **Rhythm Track:** #5 **Technique:** Arpeggios **Genre:** Any

Description: The V(#9) (dominant #9) is a cool chord to use in your playing. If you continue building thirds beyond the seventh, the next note (B, in this example) is referred to as a ninth. A #9 just raises that note by a half step, in this case to B#. In terms of fingering this pitch, it's probably easier to think of that note as a C.

Tip: To play the triple stops in the last bar, get your fingers set and aim the bow toward the D string, almost over the fingerboard where the string angle is flatter. Once you feel comfortable with the chord voicing at the end of the exercise, try playing it in a different key.

FRI

Workout #355 **Rhythm Track:** #1 **Technique:** Playing with Others **Genre:** Latin

Description: Here's another montuno commonly found in Latin tunes. If you like this sound, check out some salsa music. You might enjoy listening to Eddie Palmieri.

Tip: Try playing everything with your thumb in guitar position. Make the eighth notes pop out and keep them short by quickly releasing the pressure of your left hand.

SAT

Workout #356 **Rhythm Track:** #5 **Technique:** Bowing **Genre:** Any

Description: Earlier in the book, we played a string-crossing exercise similar to this. Now we're going to add some left-hand interest and crank up the tempo.

Tip: It may help you to put small accents on each beat. Stay with the click.

SUN

Workout #357 **Rhythm Track:** #4 **Technique:** Stretching Out **Genre:** Blues/Swing

About the Example: Swing hard and make Stuff Smith proud!

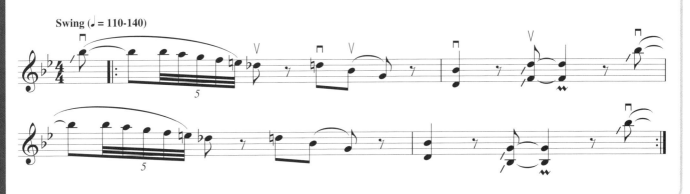

Workout #358   **Rhythm Track:** #2   **Technique:** Scales   **Genre:** Any

Description: Scales can be an endless source of material to practice. When you need a break from practicing more common double stops like thirds and sixths, try something unusual like this scale played in seconds.

Tip: Pay close attention to your intonation and to whether the interval is a minor or major second. There are two pairs of pitches a half step apart (between the third and fourth notes and between the seventh and eighth), just like in every major scale.

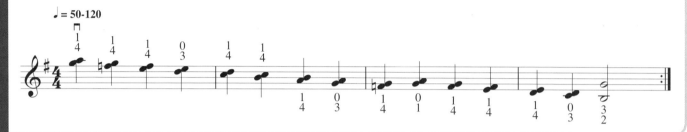

Workout #359   **Rhythm Track:** #2   **Technique:** Ornaments   **Genre:** Any pop style

Description: A cool timbral change is part of harmonics' charm. Let's alternate between two pitches, each played two ways.

Tip: The harmonics in this exercise are played high up on the G string. The harmonics are the same pitches as the stopped notes on the E string. You'll have a big shift back and forth between the two versions of each pitch.

Workout #360   **Rhythm Track:** #2   **Technique:** Rhythm/Feel   **Genre:** Any

Description: You may find this example difficult to play quickly, especially with this bowing. Such passages are the bane of orchestras everywhere!

Tip: Start practicing slowly, listening closely to the click of your metronome. As you increase the tempo, think in larger groupings of notes. Be sure to stay focused on the sound of the click.

THU

Workout #361   **Rhythm Track:** #4   **Technique:** Arpeggios   **Genre:** Any

Description: The most common chord pattern in jazz is the ii-V (pronounced "two-five"). In music theory, lower-case Roman numerals are minor chords; upper-case numerals are major chords. In jazz, the basic structure of chords is the four-note 7th chord rather than a three-note triad. This exercise is a pattern of descending, arpeggiated ii-V chords with four notes for each chord.

Tip: The first four notes spell out a C#min7 chord, the second four notes an F#7 chord. Then the pattern repeats a half step lower (Cm7, F7) and so on. Try continuing this descending sequence all the way down the violin's range.

FRI

Workout #362   **Rhythm Track:** #2   **Technique:** Playing with Others   **Genre:** Funk

Description: A lot of funk revolves around repeated two- and four-bar figures. This exercise is a riff similar to what a funk rhythm guitarist might play.

Tip: To keep the eighth and 16th notes short, you'll need to keep your strings from continuing to vibrate. Lift the fingers of your left hand slightly after the fingered notes and dampen the open strings with the left hand so that they don't keep ringing.

SAT

Workout #363   **Rhythm Track:** #5   **Technique:** Bowing   **Genre:** Any pop style

Description: These two bowings are tricky, but they sound cool and can be a way to add more variety to your chop-style rhythm figures. There's little lateral movement of the bow; it's mostly vertical. There's only a hint of an up- or down-bow.

Tip: To play these bowings, the tempo needs to be quick enough to allow the bow to ricochet in your hand as you play close to the frog. Employ the same hand position that you used on the chop exercises. This exercise is meant as a beginning point to encourage you to experiment with different chopping techniques of your own.

SUN

Workout #364   **Rhythm Track:** #1   **Technique:** Stretching Out   **Genre:** Funk/Pop

About the Example: This etude marries two bars of a common funk guitar voicing with four bars of a 7/8 riff.

MON

Workout #365 **Rhythm Track:** #2 **Technique:** Stretching Out **Genre:** Funk
About the Example: Let's put together a bunch of the funk concepts we've worked on this year.

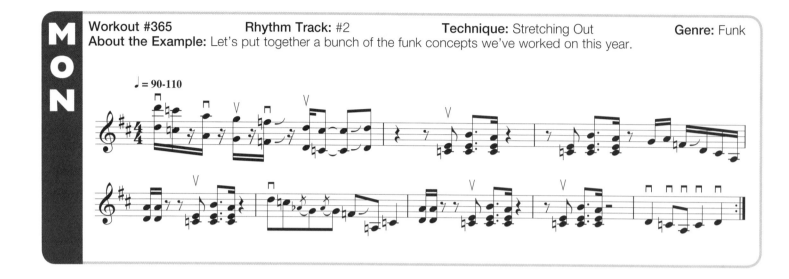

ACKNOWLEDGMENTS

I want to thank Holly Bobula for all her feedback and patience; Jake Johnson for his golden ears and for being such a pleasure to work with; my parents Jim and Jane for their endless understanding and support. I'd also like to express my deep gratitude to Tyrone Greive, Gunther Schuller, David Miotke, and Matt Glaser – all great musicians and teachers.

ABOUT THE AUTHOR

Jon Vriesacker is a musician with significant experience in a wide range of musical styles. He has worked with dozens of bands performing many genres, from bluegrass and jazz to rock and funk. He started playing when he was five, after hearing a performance of Ravel's *String Quartet in F Major*. By the time he was ten, he was winning fiddle contests and had joined a band of older musicians after teaching himself to improvise. As a teenager, his idea of what the violin could do changed when his mother brought home a Jean-Luc Ponty album.

Vriesacker studied jazz with Matt Glaser at the Berklee College of Music in Boston, received a degree in classical violin at the University of Wisconsin-Madison, and is a member of the Madison Symphony Orchestra. He has soloed with the Smithsonian Jazz Masterworks Orchestra and has worked with Pulitzer Prize-winning composer Gunther Schuller. Jon has been featured with violin legends Johnny Frigo and Johnny Gimble and has played on promotional materials for Lands' End and Miller Brewing. He can be heard on recordings by Willy Porter, Freedy Johnston, and Garbage. Vriesacker also played on "Al Otro Lado del Rio," from the movie *The Motorcycle Diaries*, which won an Academy Award for Best Original Song in 2005. He lives in Madison, Wisconsin.

The Violin Play-Along Series

Play your favorite songs quickly and easily!

Just follow the music, listen to the CD or online audio to hear how the violin should sound, and then play along using the separate backing tracks. The audio files are enhanced so you can adjust the recordings to any tempo without changing pitch!

  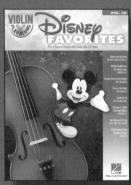  

1. Bluegrass
00842152 Book/CD Pack $14.99

2. Popular Songs
00842153 Book/CD Pack $14.99

3. Classical
00842154 Book/CD Pack $14.99

4. Celtic
00842155 Book/CD Pack $14.99

5. Christmas Carols
00842156 Book/CD Pack $14.99

6. Holiday Hits
00842157 Book/CD Pack $14.99

7. Jazz
00842196 Book/CD Pack $14.99

8. Country Classics
00842230 Book/CD Pack $12.99

9. Country Hits
00842231 Book/CD Pack $14.99

10. Bluegrass Favorites
00842232 Book/CD Pack $14.99

11. Bluegrass Classics
00842233 Book/CD Pack $14.99

12. Wedding Classics
00842324 Book/CD Pack $14.99

13. Wedding Favorites
00842325 Book/CD Pack $14.99

14. Blues Classics
00842427 Book/CD Pack $14.99

15. Stephane Grappelli
00842428 Book/CD Pack $14.99

16. Folk Songs
00842429 Book/CD Pack $14.99

17. Christmas Favorites
00842478 Book/CD Pack $14.99

18. Fiddle Hymns
00842499 Book/CD Pack $14.99

19. Lennon & McCartney
00842564 Book/CD Pack $14.99

20. Irish Tunes
00842565 Book/CD Pack $14.99

21. Andrew Lloyd Webber
00842566 Book/CD Pack $14.99

22. Broadway Hits
00842567 Book/CD Pack $14.99

23. Pirates of the Caribbean
00842625 Book/CD Pack $14.99

24. Rock Classics
00842640 Book/CD Pack $14.99

25. Classical Masterpieces
00842642 Book/CD Pack $14.99

26. Elementary Classics
00842643 Book/CD Pack $14.99

27. Classical Favorites
00842646 Book/CD Pack $14.99

28. Classical Treasures
00842647 Book/CD Pack $14.99

29. Disney Favorites
00842648 Book/CD Pack $14.99

30. Disney Hits
00842649 Book/CD Pack $14.99

31. Movie Themes
00842706 Book/CD Pack $14.99

32. Favorite Christmas Songs
00102110 Book/CD Pack $14.99

33. Hoedown
00102161 Book/CD Pack $14.99

34. Barn Dance
00102568 Book/CD Pack $14.99

35. Lindsey Stirling
00109715 Book/CD Pack $19.99

36. Hot Jazz
00110373 Book/CD Pack $14.99

37. Taylor Swift
00116361 Book/CD Pack $14.99

38. John Williams
00116367 Book/CD Pack $14.99

39. Italian Songs
00116368 Book/CD Pack $14.99

41. Johann Strauss
00121041 Book/CD Pack $14.99

42. Light Classics
00121935 Book/Online Audio $14.99

43. Light Orchestra Pop
00122126 Book/Online Audio $14.99

44. French Songs
00122123 Book/Online Audio $14.99

45. Lindsey Stirling Hits
00123128 Book/Online Audio $19.99

47. Light Masterworks
00124149 Book/Online Audio $14.99

48. Frozen
00126478 Book/Online Audio $14.99

49. Pop/Rock
00130216 Book/Online Audio $14.99

50. Songs For Beginners
00131417 Book/Online Audio $14.99

51. Chart Hits For Beginners
00131418 Book/Online Audio $14.99

Disney characters and artwork © Disney Enterprises, Inc.
Prices, contents, and availability
subject to change without notice.

HAL•LEONARD®
CORPORATION
7777 W. BLUEMOUND RD. P.O. BOX 13819 MILWAUKEE, WI 53213

www.halleonard.com

0315